Praise for

THE FIVE CONVERSATIONS ABOUT MONEY THAT WILL RADICALLY CHANGE YOUR LIFE

"Vanessa is a natural storyteller. Strong. Relatable. Purpose driven."

—Business in Heels

"Vanessa Stoykov is the 'Oprah of Money'... She knows how important it is to have courageous conversations in order to achieve financial freedom."

—Saxton Speakers Bureau

"Vanessa has brilliantly depicted the many and varied relationships we all have with money and work through her characters and insights. You're going to recognise everyone in her book, and realise that we can all 'unlearn' poor habits. This is relatable and engaging storytelling."

—Sally Loane, former ABC broadcaster and CEO

"There is no better way than talking to tackle the subject of money—but how do you start? When do you have them? What do you ask? And who should you be having a conversation with? Vanessa Stoykov provides you with the right money conversations for your life—best kept on the middle shelf of your bookcase so it is always available when you need it!"

—Pauline Vamos, chair and board director

"Vanessa Stoykov cares about helping people achieve their life goals and financial wellbeing. In this book she provides practical tips on how you can make that happen and discussions you should be having. She does this in a down-to-earth, easy-to-read way that will have you relating to her characters, laughing and making you think and take action. If you want to get ahead, read it!"

—Julie Lander, CEO of CareSuper

"There's so much more to effectively managing your money than just budgeting, and this book is a timely reminder of that. Whether you've got a little or a lot, Vanessa will help you understand and take control of your money to help you build a happier future."

—Kylie Merritt, Ausbiz TV

"Incredibly valuable and eye-opening. It felt like I was inside honest conversations throughout the book. It was full of aha moments and practical ways to deal with money issues I'd been avoiding. It was personal, genuine, and has inspired me to open up about what was once taboo. The most insightful read around how money can help you live a better life."

—Kim Payne, founder of 9rok

THE FIVE CONVERSATIONS ABOUT MONEY THAT WILL RADICALLY CHANGE YOUR LIFE

THE FIVE CONVERSATIONS ABOUT MONEY THAT WILL RADICALLY CHANGE YOUR LIFE

Could Be the Best Money Book
You Ever Own

Vanessa Stoykov

mango
PUBLISHING GROUP

CORAL GABLES

Copyright © 2022 by Vanessa Stoykov.
Published by Mango Publishing, a division of Mango Publishing
Group, Inc.

Cover Design: Scott McNamara
Layout & Design: Scott McNamara

Mango is an active supporter of authors' rights to free
speech and artistic expression in their books. The purpose
of copyright is to encourage authors to produce exceptional
works that enrich our culture and our open society.

Uploading or distributing photos, scans or any content from
this book without prior permission is theft of the author's
intellectual property. Please honor the author's work as you
would your own. Thank you in advance for respecting our
author's rights.

For permission requests, please contact the publisher at:
Mango Publishing Group
2850 S Douglas Road, 4th Floor
Coral Gables, FL 33134 USA
info@mango.bz

For special orders, quantity sales, course adoptions and
corporate sales, please email the publisher at sales@mango.
bz. For trade and wholesale sales, please contact Ingram
Publisher Services at customer.service@ingramcontent.com or
+1.800.509.4887.

The Five Conversations about Money that Will Radically
Change Your Life: Could Be the Best Money Book You
Ever Own

Library of Congress Cataloging-in-Publication number:
2022940948
ISBN: (p) 978-1-68481-024-6, (e) 978-1-68481-025-3
BISAC category code BUS027020, BUSINESS & ECONOMICS
/ Finance / Financial Risk Management

Printed in the United States of America

**Everybody has a money story.
Start talking about yours today. See how your life changes.**

Vanessa Stoykov

TABLE OF CONTENTS

YOUR LIFE STORY HAS MANY CHAPTERS

Like any good book, there is always a beginning. A start to your own money story, that you play out in your mind. How you grew up. Where you are from.

Did you grow up with money? If so, how much? Did you start with nothing, or less than nothing, and fight your way through life? Whatever your story, and we will get to your story, you have formed a view of life based on the experiences you have had, and the life wisdom you have accumulated up to this point.

My hope with this book is to set you upon new chapters in your own life story, by having crucial conversations about money with the intention and purpose of creating the life you want for yourself and your family.

Money is simply a tool with which we can make choices. And choices are the things that make up our life circumstance. How we start is not necessarily how we end – it is all up to the choices we make.

I have interviewed, filmed, and written about people from all walks of life, around the common theme of money, for more than twenty-seven years. And one thing I have learned about it is that money represents a lot more about a person than their net worth.

How we value ourselves, our perception of others, and the social judgements we make are all closely tied to money. Yet it remains one of the last taboos in our society to talk openly about it.

As you go through each of the five conversations in this book (Chapter 1 is a must for those of you who skip to the end first – you know who you are), I encourage you to think about challenging your views on money by being honest with yourself. Are you happy with your life story so far?

Do you look at other people's lives with envy or regret? Are you at a point where you need to start a new chapter, but don't know how?

Or are you worried about your adult kids with money, how they are coping, or whether you can help?

Are you in a relationship that is full of unspoken friction about money?

Or are you part of a family that struggles to make ends meet and is always just coping?

Whatever chapter you are at in your own life, use this book as a source of permission to open up the conversations about money you need to have, whether with your partner, your children, or your parents. For, when you start the conversation, a whole new world of possibilities opens up.

That's my intention for you.

Vanessa Stoykov

WHY WE NEED TO TALK ABOUT MONEY

Congratulations! You have taken the first step in having courageous conversations about money just by buying this book. In a world where we'll take detours to avoid the topic, you've gone out and made a bold move to read something that's going to get you more comfortable with money and with talking about it.

There might be many reasons why you've picked up this book. Maybe you're at a point where something in your life has changed – or maybe something needs to change. This part is always a bit scary, but also exciting, because you can only get to somewhere new through growth and change.

I wrote this book with the hope that it becomes a guide you can refer to as you start to make your way through the important, yet sometimes confronting, conversations you need to have to create change for your life and to more easily navigate this thing we rely on so heavily called money.

Creating change is all about doing something differently than you have before. There are moments in all our lives where we reach flashpoints – periods of high stress, high emotion, good or bad, where something shifts, and demands that we react.

It may be the beginning, or the ending, of an important relationship. The loss of a loved one. A pandemic. The sting of failure. The sweet taste of success. Whatever your flashpoint is, the choices you make when you reach that point define your life.

After twenty-seven years of working in the finance industry, as both a finance journalist and money educator, I have developed a method of storytelling that creates what I call *financial* flashpoints, which are the catalysts around money that can spark change in your life. Financial flashpoints are moments where your need to change combines with a different way of looking at money to create an action. You can have many financial flashpoints over your lifetime – and you might even have several as you read this book.

This book is about having the right conversation starters available when these flashpoints arise, so you can make decisions based on what you really want for your life long-term.

Here's one of *my* favourite financial flashpoints. It's about when I started my business at age twenty-six.

I'm going to share it with you in the form of a podcast script. This style of storytelling is one of my favourites because I can show you the inside of a character's head. Here goes.

Vanessa, aged twenty-six. Working as business development manager for a fund manager. Earning $150,000 and driving a 3 series BMW. Wearing a Carla Zampatti suit that was bought with her bonus.

Opening scene: We see Vanessa driving her blue BMW into a basement to park in the city.

VANESSA

God, I love that I am scamming free parking in this building. I love the cool old basement guy. Other people are paying a fortune for their spots on George St. I am so lucky.

GOING UP LIFT TO WORK:

Hmm, who should I call today? I've got reporting due soon, so I have to chase some leads. I hate it when my sales reports are questioned.

GETTING OUT OF LIFT INTO THE CORRIDOR:

WTF's happening here? I can't breathe. Jeez, I am literally freaking out right now. I need to get out of here.

CUT TO BASEMENT, CRYING

I'm calling my sister and telling her I can't do my job anymore. Yet I don't really even know why I am saying that.

→

My body was telling me something I wasn't admitting to myself. I was not cut out for corporate life. I was pretending to be someone I wasn't, and it was starting to affect my mental health.

<table>
<tr><td>GETTING REAL
AFTER BEING
DRAMATIC</td><td>Take a deep breath, Stoykov. I don't need to go back. I can quit.</td></tr>
</table>

Okay, I actually did have to go back, but I gave myself permission to think about quitting.

<table>
<tr><td>VANESSA</td><td>Ringing the agency that did our advertising – "Could I work in Creative?" Finding out that a creative director earned $150,000 in advertising and she was not qualified.</td></tr>
<tr><td>VANESSA</td><td>But they offered to rent me a room in the house where their agency was located. I could start my own business.</td></tr>
<tr><td>VANESSA
OLDER NOW:</td><td>And so it began. Evolution Media Group was born, and I have never looked back.</td></tr>
</table>

This flashpoint is all about the period of my life when I decided to start my own business. In my heart I knew I was a creative, a storyteller, and that my skills were not suited to a corporate life. At my very core, I cherish freedom, family, and creativity. I wanted to include all of that in my life at once. Showing up to my office every day, no matter how great the people were, was not going to deliver on happiness for me. But it did mean I had to get smart with money, quickly. I was no longer earning a regular salary, and the $14,000 I had saved up wouldn't last long. The series of events that happened after that were all a product of that big flashpoint I had, where I no longer wanted the life I had built for myself. The life I had thought would make me happy.

Here's what I know about people when it comes to money. Most people don't care about spreadsheets or investing. What they do want to know is how they can retire comfortably, or live in their dream home, or buy the car they really want. They want to bring their kids up with a solid education and have no debt to their name, while enjoying family holidays. They don't want to face Monday morning with a major headache and a list of tasks that seems insurmountable.

Ultimately, people want happiness and security. The thing is, you can't avoid money if you want that kind of life. Money, with the right mindset, is the bridge to your dream life. It's the jam that makes the bread stick together. It enables you to make the choices you really want, not the ones you *have* to make.

MONEY BUYS YOU FREEDOM TO CHOOSE HOW TO SPEND YOUR TIME.

Many of us turn a blind eye to money simply because we're embarrassed to talk about it, or admit our own financial situation. The reason for this is deep, and part of it comes from old childhood beliefs.

Money can be confusing and complex, and can also be intimidating and anxiety-inducing, especially when you don't have enough for the everyday of life, let alone the bigger things. It can make us feel like we haven't achieved, or don't know as much as other people about making it.

Could this be why we're not willing to talk about this stuff called money? Hmm, well, yes.

I'm here to get you thinking about money in a new way, by sparking courageous conversations that get us talking about what we all really want in life and finding the most direct route to get it. The more we talk openly about money, the faster we will kill the stigma attached to it, which, frankly, is getting us nowhere.

> **IT'S TIME TO GET REAL ABOUT MONEY, LOSE THE TABOOS, AND START TALKING ABOUT WHAT WE REALLY WANT FROM LIFE.**

FACING THE FEAR
AROUND MONEY

I'm all about having authentic conversations about money, because this is where real change starts. It's where we confront our demons and get to the nitty-gritty of what's really going on. It allows us to confront our own stories about money and to put everything out on the table – in a room where we leave shame and embarrassment at the door. You can only do this if you're okay with being real with yourself and those around you.

Social conditioning has made money a taboo subject, and that has made a lot of us feel like we can't and shouldn't talk about money. It prevents us from confronting it, talking about it with those closest to us, including our kids, parents, siblings, friends, and coworkers. Some of us can't even talk to our own partners about money, even if we share bills, a mortgage, kids' school fees and a bed with them.

Our conditioning is so deeply rooted in us that we don't even realise it's there half the time. It's what you picked up from your parents or family members when you were growing up. It's the lack of talking about it at school and at home, and it's what we pick up from our friends. It's the stories we've heard over and over again that we now need to unlearn.

It's often too hard to face our own dirty laundry when it comes to money. We'd do anything to avoid the conversation about our financial situation, so we just keep on living a life that's not really what we want because we don't want to confront it. But confronting it is the only way to make real change.

In this book we are going to crack open these conversations, so you can start talking about the things that matter with one clear end goal in sight

TALKING OPENLY, WITHOUT FEAR OR SHAME, ABOUT MONEY WILL SET YOU UP TO LIVE A HAPPIER LIFE, INSPIRED TO TAKE POSITIVE ACTION TOWARD YOUR OWN FINANCIAL FUTURE.

BY RECOGNISING YOUR OWN FINANCIAL FLASHPOINTS, YOU CAN TAKE THE STEPS NEEDED TO MAKE A CHANGE. THIS IS A LIFELONG JOURNEY OF UNDERSTANDING THE POWER OF TALKING AND THINKING DIFFERENTLY ABOUT MONEY.

IT ALSO MEANS YOU WILL HAVE A HEALTHIER DIALOGUE ABOUT MONEY WITH THOSE AROUND YOU EVERY DAY.

It's obvious why a person's well-being improves when they don't need to stress about money. Have you ever experienced financial stress when the stakes are high? The fear and dread attached to those moments in your life are significant and can have real impact on your mental health.

It's so fundamental to our lives – it puts food on the table, clothes on our back, a home to live in, and access to education and the lifestyle we want. For some people, it's the difference between being able to sleep at night or not, or the difference between getting up in the morning ready to face the day with optimism or staring down a barrel of dread. I am all about the good night's sleep and the feeling that you and your family are going to be okay when it comes to money.

OPENING THE CONVERSATION

The financial stress we've seen since the pandemic has taken a devastating toll on many people and businesses, and it has put strain on governments. But it's worth noting that this pandemic and the economic shift that has come from it also comes at the time of the greatest global wealth transfer in history. Right now, and in the coming decades, trillions of dollars are being handed down from baby boomers to the next generation. Every major country in the world is seeing a massive intergenerational handover in the trillions.

I've been talking about the intergenerational wealth transfer in the media for years, and for good reason – it's going to be a massive game-changer; what we do with this money has the potential to influence our future prosperity for generations to come.

There are trillions of dollars changing hands here in Australia and around the globe. It's going to change things for people personally, as well as for the greater economy – but only if we know how to invest this windfall in an impactful way. As a collective, we need to be ready to take positive action, and that's partly why we need to be comfortable talking about money in a radically new way.

It starts with being courageous and having confronting conversations you've probably been avoiding – with your partner, parents, siblings, kids, and especially yourself. It means finally talking with your parents about inheritance if it's been on your mind, so you can prepare for what's to come or initiating the conversation with your adult children.

Now, before you shut the book because you don't want to confront any of this stuff, hang in there with me. Even if you don't have any of these conversations with anyone else, getting real with yourself is the most important part. Obviously, I'd like you to start getting comfortable talking about money with the people around you and those closest to you – but only as long as you can be true with yourself about money first, because that's what matters more than anything.

This book will help you have the conversations you need to make some serious shifts in your money story. Having real conversations about money can give you and everyone around you the opportunity to experience those financial flashpoints, the lightbulb moments that will spark you to take action to make your life better.

It doesn't matter what stage you're at in your life now, the state of your current finances, where you want to go, or how impossible it all feels – now is the time to start. You've already taken the first step by opening this book. Having curiosity and a willingness to know more and do more means you are on your way to creating a different kind of life for yourself and your family. To get the most from your investment in this book, be honest with yourself when thinking about the ideas I ask you to consider. By doing that, you'll learn the steps and conversations you need to create the intentional financial life you want for yourself and your family.

If you follow this process and are courageous enough to have these conversations, I guarantee your life will change for the better. I believe we all deserve a less stressful life. It's time to invest in yourself and your future. There's no better time to start than now.

Okay, let's chat.

Chapter 1

THE RAW + HONEST CONVERSATION YOU NEED TO HAVE WITH YOURSELF

1

ASK YOURSELF WHAT YOU REALLY WANT IN LIFE—AND WHAT'S STOPPING YOU FROM GETTING IT.

If there's one part of this book I want you to focus on more than anything, it's this. Everything starts with you when it comes to money. I want you to walk away with this first conversation under your belt. (It's the most important one because, when it comes to anything in life, you've got to start with you.)

This conversation will build the foundation from the ground up – not just your financial well-being, but the basis for the life you really want to be living. Figuring out what you want and don't want in life, being able to change how you think about what you can have, and taking steps in the right direction to help get you there, all starts with you.

You might think it's not quite normal to be having a conversation with yourself. But, in my opinion, it's crazy not to. Having conversations with yourself means giving yourself valuable time to reflect on what you truly want in your life.

Over time, we've learned to put ourselves second and others first – our kids, partner, parents, job, and other responsibilities tend to get the best of us. Yes, it's important to prioritise all these people and things that are closest to us. But there comes a point in our lives where we start to treat ourselves like observers sitting on the sidelines. Even if everyone around you demands a lot of you, you've got to make time for knowing yourself again. If you've forgotten that you are the most important player in your own life, I'm here to remind you.

Easy for you to say, the bills have to be paid or we don't eat.

ME IN YOUR HEAD

You are essential. This is true. But you also deserve to be happy.

YOU

I would be if I had more money. Me talking about it won't make that happen.

ME IN YOUR HEAD

How much do you need? Exactly.

YOU

Hmmm. Let me think about that.

ME IN YOUR HEAD

Ha. So now you are figuring out your number. Name your price.

YOU

OK. How much do I need to be happy?

So there you have it. The big question right up front. What's it really going to take to make your life the way you really want? Enough to never have to work? To give each of your kids a home? To buy a roof over your head and groceries for life? What's your idea of the perfect life, and what would that cost? By making this the first conversation this book guides you through, we really start with what matters to you the most.

I guess I'm still a product of my 1973 birthday, because whenever I get asked that, I always want to say "one million dollars" in a Schwarzenegger-style accent. The reality is that most people don't go around knowing their "number," and it takes more than five minutes to cost out your life. And, most likely, it will be more than a million dollars, if you get real about what life costs nowadays.

You could take the time to do the quick math on your phone or piece of paper. If you live to be ninety, what's that life gonna look like? What would that cost? I am forty years away from that, so my number would have to pay for forty more good living years. What's it going to cost per year of your life? That's your number. If I say $100,000 a year for life, which doesn't seem too greedy for my dream life, times forty years of living, that equals four million dollars. Maybe that's why we don't dream out loud more as we get older. Because those numbers sound too big. Unachievable. Pipe dream stuff.

> **THIS CONVERSATION IS ABOUT LETTING GO OF WHAT YOU THINK YOU ARE CAPABLE OF ACHIEVING. FORGETTING ABOUT WHAT OTHERS THINK, AND PEOPLE YOU SEE ON SOCIAL MEDIA. IT IS ABOUT ASKING YOURSELF: WHAT REALLY MATTERS TO ME?**

UNLEARNING WHAT YOU'VE LEARNED

It's time to confront your relationship with money, how you identify with it, and what you've been telling yourself about it all along.

I've spent my life having conversations with people about money. In talking with them, I've found that everyone has their own story around money. Whether it's positive or negative, it's a powerful narrative that people hold onto to help them feel in control or to justify why they aren't in control of their own lives. But they don't have to believe these stories and beliefs.

My first book, *The Breakfast Club for 40-Somethings*, is a chronicle of the lives of six people in their mid-forties who go to their twenty-five-year high school reunion. Secrets start to unravel when they gather in the old gym, after a few drinks to loosen up their nerves. As they start to reconnect, they each reveal what their lives are actually like beneath the surface. They certainly aren't what they appear to be on social media, and there were some pretty heavy confessions around the reality of each of their lives.

Luckily for them, the all-round good guy from their year, Ben, walks into the gym. He listens to all their confessions about what life is really like, and he starts to make an assessment. A lot of the pressures, stress, and unhappiness they are experiencing have financial implications.

Ben is a financial planner who has considerable emotional intelligence. He taps into those implications to explain how their behaviour is creating the problems. He calls it "unlearning money," and takes them through five pillars to show them how to identify what it is that each of them needs to unlearn. Ben shows them it is what they know about money that is holding them back. They have to change their mindset in order to change their situation. But first, they have to look back on their lives to understand where their beliefs began. With Ben's guidance, all the characters go through a process of unlearning what they picked up about money that was holding them back, which is a process I find a lot of people go through as we get older.

Karen and Russ, who were married with three kids, had to unlearn their childhood beliefs and expectations around who should be the breadwinner. Single Mum Jane coped with her dreams of a happy marriage and perfect life not working out, and perennial party boy Jasper, who had a long-term habit of hitting his mum up for money, had to find financial independence. Josie learned how to extricate herself from a business that relied too heavily on her, while billionaire Brad realised that people are the most important component of any happy life, not money and success.

If you want to know more about what Ben told them, you can find out more or listen to my podcast at the end of this book.

The characters were created to represent people we all know. (Except perhaps Brad. He is almost too good to be true.) They are working on the school canteen, selling you cars, or doing your taxes. The thing they all have in common is that they were making decisions about money based on where they *were*, not where they wanted to be.

I'll be using one of my storytelling genres to make this money book more interesting. In each chapter I will include a script, with the characters and their money conversations front and centre. From this, you will understand the lessons learned by each of the characters, and what most applies to you and your life. I will also be including you as a character in my conversation bubble scripts as we go through the conversations, so you can play them out in your head.

Today our breakfast club characters are reflecting on their own lives and where they are at.

KAREN

Before kids, I never had a goal for myself. I never really went for it. Never thought I could. So what am I supposed to do when the kids go? (*Imagine a Reese Witherspoon cute mama role*)

JOSIE

My work is my baby. If I don't put in the hours, things will fall through the cracks. I'm getting tired, but I rarely let it show. (*An elegant Angelina Jolie type with a sad air*)

JASPER

I'm getting pretty sick of living with Mum. I feel like everyone else is grown up except me. It's hard to even get a lease now. (*Vince Vaughan with a rough-around-the-edges twist. Charismatic, but a little faded*)

RUSS

I'm expected to get results at work, but half my team won't come back to the office since the pandemic. My job is much more stressful than it was pre-COVID. I don't feel secure. And I'm sick of trying to keep everyone that works for me positive. (*Jason Bateman looks and manner, with conservative dress sense*)

JANE

Mum and Dad are finding it harder to mind the girls. I need to juggle work and pick them up from after-school care. My life is pick up and drop off and work. Thank god for Netflix and nine o'clock bedtime. (*Think Jennifer Garner, genuine, capable, shy*)

In midlife, money and the need to pursue it can be overwhelming and exhausting. Admitting where you are at is essential. Remember that comparing ourselves to others can be a grind that causes us to keep problems hidden and only show the best parts of our lives on social media...which is what everyone else is also doing.

Like the characters in my book, unlearning some of the beliefs you have accumulated about money and putting your energy into creating a purposeful plan for the life you really want, can dramatically increase your chances of getting what you want out of life. It's the first step you can take toward putting yourself front and centre and planning the life you really want for yourself and your family in the future.

FINANCIAL FLASHPOINTS

You're going to hear me talk about financial flashpoints a lot. As you face money challenges at different stages in your life, you'll have little epiphanies along the way that will help you figure out your next step. This has happened throughout my entire life. After a quarter of a century of working in the money industry, I've had many financial flashpoints that have served as moments of realisation, whether that was for my business, or my personal life. We have sold our home to fund our business, moved to the Blue Mountains for five years to raise our sons, and took turns being breadwinners. Each change was made in moments of crisis or opportunity, where we really had to think deeply about what was making us happy, and what was not.

You're going to have lots of financial flashpoints for yourself as you read this book, and it will be like turning on a lightbulb in your brain that will direct you to make changes that will lead to better outcomes for your life in the future. They'll spark you to think differently and spur you on to take action that will move you toward the life you really want.

These little insights will come up as you ask yourself the important questions, and they will continue as you start talking about money with the people closest to you.

You might have plenty of financial flashpoints as you get through this book, or maybe just one big one that's been eager to come out. But it won't stop at today. They'll keep happening throughout your life. Your opportunity is to make choices at that point that lead to long-term change for the better.

IT STARTS WITH YOUR
MONEY MINDSET

Money is a big part of my life. I've worked in financial services for a long time, and I've created and produced stories alongside seriously wealthy people, from millionaires to billionaires. It's opened my eyes to the world of money, and a new way of thinking about it. What have I learned from these finance experts about money? Well, it is not about how much money you have or how much you earn; it's about how you think about money and what it can do for you. It's about making money work for you with your actions and behaviours, and this all starts with having the right money mindset.

What I've come to realise is that with the right mindset there's always a way forward – and often what comes out of a financial blunder can be an even bigger and better opportunity than you could have imagined. And that lesson you gained is far more valuable than you might think. Money mistakes can cause us grief, but there's always an opportunity to grow from them. And, like financial flashpoints, mistakes are going to happen, and they're a catalyst that will set you in a new direction.

I've been told more money secrets that I could recall about mistakes people have made. But I've also seen how possible it is to start from zero (or from minus zero – that is, debt) and build financial confidence and security from next to nothing.

I have also learned this: The only way to pick yourself up and out of a financial slump and move toward the life you want to be living is by *changing your mindset*.

> **EVEN YOUR BIGGEST FAILURES CAN BE OPPORTUNITIES FOR GROWTH, AND THAT'S WHAT HAVING A GROWTH MINDSET IS ABOUT.**

CHALLENGING YOUR BELIEFS ABOUT MONEY

Money, or lack of it, is not what holds us back in life. It is our deep-rooted beliefs that stop us from doing what we're capable of. Do you believe that you never have enough? That money slips right through your fingers? That you can never earn enough? What we inherently believe about money usually turns out to be true.

Your money mindset starts way back in childhood. It's conditioned in us by society and the people we surround ourselves with, including our family. It keeps us in a loop of what we think we "should" be doing. It's the things we do and say on autopilot because that's "just the way it is."

Some people stay in unhappy marriages, or remain tied to a mortgage they don't want anymore because they feel they can't get out of it. Many people stay in jobs for years, or even decades, because they think it's too late to make a change or that it's all they are capable of. You might assume you wouldn't know how to navigate the stock market or understand investing. But you've got to ask yourself, is what you're thinking really true?

It's amazing how we limit ourselves just by our beliefs. It's never too late or impossible to challenge your beliefs or make a radical change in your life, even if you think there are things holding you back. But you've got to be willing to confront what's going on and get comfortable with the uncomfortable.

A lot of us could be doing more when it comes to money and life. We could probably be in a better financial situation, living a life that's truer to what we really want – if only we allowed ourselves to go there or knew which bridge to cross. You might think you could never have or be what you really want, but here's where we're going to start challenging those limiting beliefs.

HERE'S THE THING: YOU GET WHAT (YOU THINK) YOU DESERVE.

Opens on Jasper and Russ sitting at the bar of the local bowling club, having a beer.

JASPER
I've had it with that place. My commission went to that old guy who swanned in at the last second. I saw that couple last week and sold that car. I'm sick of getting screwed for money.

RUSS
What's your base at that job? You seem pretty angry about a one-off car commission.

JASPER
The base is nothing. Five hundred dollars a week. It's just lucky I don't pay rent at Mum's, let's just say.

RUSS
Mate, you can do better. I know you can.

JASPER
Yeah, well, my ship hasn't come in yet. We can't all be tie-wearing money makers like you.

RUSS
Yeah, noose-wearing more like it. Another week of ten-hour days with people off sick and not doing their job. Living the dream.

While each of them has very different problems, neither is enjoying the way they make money. It's only when they both change their mindset that things start to change.

Sometimes opening up about life and sharing what it's really like can be cathartic. But the best conversations about money also include possible ways forward. Complaining to friends is one thing, but that only gets you so far.

It's possible to create the life you want for the next stage, instead of settling for what you've got. Life is too short to settle for anything less. We have a limited amount of time on this earth and endless potential to make something of our lives and create a legacy. How can you make the most of it?

Scene opens on Josie and Karen at a coffee shop in the mall, mainly looking at things for Josie.

KAREN

Thank god for coffee. My one true love. Do you know it's the thing I think about first when I open my eyes?

JOSIE

Really? I'm thinking about my diary the minute I wake up; go to the gym, then get in to work. It's only then I'll have a coffee.

KAREN

That's because you have discipline. I have none. And I'm always running around getting the kids ready for school. It's my fuel.

JOSIE

I don't know how you do it with three. You are amazing.

KAREN

I think you are amazing. The hours you work and what you achieve.

$\longrightarrow$

JOSIE	Thanks, babe. Although I'm starting to feel different about it all. Like I'm living Groundhog Day. I wonder what it would be like to wake up to kids. Or to a life that isn't on permanent GO.
KAREN	I've never heard you talk like that. Interesting. Not a bad thought, old friend.
JOSIE	Well, I guess closing in on fifty makes you wonder how much you really have left.
KAREN	God, I constantly dread the kids leaving and me still at home. I dream about getting out and about. And being part of life again. But then, what could I do?
JOSIE	Plenty. I've been thinking about this for ages. Let's talk.

Once you reassess your mindset around money and really decide what you want from this one life, your thinking around money, and what you need to know, become clearer.

BEING GOOD WITH MONEY IS MORE THAN UNDERSTANDING INVESTING AND BUDGETS. IT STARTS WITH HOW YOU THINK AND FEEL.

MAKING THE SHIFT
WHAT DO YOU WANT NOW?

Get Clear about Your "Why"

As I walk around the city, I see a lot of stressed-out faces. I know people are really feeling the pressure of the daily grind while sitting under mounds of debt and a massive mortgage. Not only are we trying to navigate a pandemic and a changing world, but we're also trying to keep up with bills and make sure we can put food on the table as prices for groceries, fuel, and other everyday needs continue to rise.

We're working hard to afford the lifestyles (we thought) we wanted, while many of us feel we can only fit in family time in moments. We are so busy doing life that we get the most pleasure looking at our lives in photos, in moments on social media, to remind ourselves how amazing it all is. To be honest, sometimes I can't even remember many of the moments I have taken pics of over the years – so I am glad I have always been an obsessive photo person, even before phones.

It's also gotten pretty scary since COVID. Will we ever feel as secure as we did before then? Our collective anxiety levels have gone up. Self-medication has become a way of coping, and for the first time in my life, I acknowledged the anxiety I have suffered from since my early twenties.

It was a pivotal flashpoint in my life. I remember my hands shaking on the steering wheel while driving home from dropping my kids off at school. It was before we went into a second, much longer lockdown. I knew I was not going to be able to drive, and had to find a way to get off a busy freeway to pull over.

Anyone who has ever suffered a panic attack while driving knows that complete terror as you lose the ability to be in control at that moment (it ain't pretty). I spoke to my GP of eighteen years, who put me on anxiety medication, which was a game-changer in helping me think more clearly. I know I am not alone in my struggle with anxiety.

It's actually been great to see mental health more openly discussed as we all face challenges together. While science can help us with feelings of depression and anxiety, there are no meds for money worries besides taking actions and having conversations you may never have had before. But this flashpoint did make me see that I needed more control over my life, my work, and what I spent my time on. I also needed to stop commuting an hour and a half to work and live closer to the action. This flashpoint caused me to reassess what I wanted. I then of course had to go and talk to my husband, and think about our entire family. How we paid for this change was a part of it, but the bigger conversation was about the life we each wanted to be living.

What most of us want in life – such as freedom, more family time, or security – is possible. Getting there starts with listing all the things we are spending the majority of our time – and our money – on now. By then looking at happiness levels associated with each, you can start to create a true picture of your everyday life versus what you want to be doing. What did I want? More time working from home and less time in the car. More catch-up with friends and less wasting time on chores that bring no joy.

It can start as simply as this. It doesn't have to be a grand plan. Just list what you want more of, and what you want less of. You can start to think about the financial implications for these things after you list what truly brings you joy.

I have created a micro course for you if you want to take it further. It's a short guide called "Building Your Dream Life," and you can find it on my website, which is referenced at the end of this book. By spending the time on figuring out what is and isn't working for you, you can start to build a future that contains more of the good stuff, and less of what you are not enjoying.

Seeing a Future That's Better Than This One
To see a future that could be even better than the one you have now, first you've got to imagine something better

than what's happening now. You need to have a belief that things can absolutely be better for you, even if it doesn't seem like it now – even if you don't quite know how to get from A to B just yet.

You might already be happy in your life, or maybe you're sitting on a minefield of catastrophe that could blow up at any moment. Maybe you don't want to rock the boat in your life or your relationships, so you stay exactly where you are. Or perhaps you are ready to wipe the slate clean and have a fresh, new start.

When you've hit a point where you're feeling stuck financially, it can seem like there's no way out of the situation. You might have piled up debt or don't have a cent to your name after years of work, or maybe you've lost a lot of money in your business, investing, or buying things you thought you wanted, or even gambling.

> **TURNING IT AROUND STARTS WITH ASKING YOURSELF TWO SIMPLE QUESTIONS: "WHAT DO I REALLY WANT FROM MY LIFE MOVING FORWARD?" AND "WHAT CAN I CHANGE TO GET WHAT I WANT?"**

Whatever has happened in your life up until this point, you can either believe where you are is the best you can do and there is nothing better coming your way, or you can start to shift your mindset to believe there is more. You can take what you've learned from experience and start from exactly where you are. What you build has the potential to be even better than you could have ever imagined, if you allow yourself to shift how you think.

When you believe there is something better for you, that's
when you can start taking positive steps to make real changes.

I come from a small country town in New South Wales
called Gunnedah. My father was an immigrant from
Eastern Europe and worked in the coal mines as a
machinist, while my mum stayed home and looked after
us. She also managed the household finances. It was an
ideal country upbringing, and while there was no spare
money to throw around, we grew up with everything we
needed. We always had food on the table, nice clothes, an
education, and an annual beachside holiday.

The biggest competitive advantage I had when I was
growing up was a belief my parents instilled in me that I
could be anything I wanted. It's this belief that drove me
forward once I left home to find my own way in the world.
At eighteen, I left to go to university in the city; in my early
twenties, I became a finance journalist in Sydney. I saw
an opportunity to bring creativity to a technical industry,
and started my own communications company at the
age of twenty-six, with $14,000 capital. I often tell people
that I spent $10,000 of that on the launch party, and in
all honesty I did. But I also invited a bunch of experts to
speak to my audience about what they did, and they paid
me to be there. And it got me my first client.

Knowing when to invest in my ideas and how to
monetise them has been a journey for me – I've sold two
businesses, the first being my PR firm, and then my online
learning platform for financial advisers. Each time, I've
learned a lot about business, about money, and, most
importantly, about what drives me.

Funnily enough, it's never really been about the
money for me in my work. (Although of course I like to be
paid.) It started by being part of an industry that I admired,
respected, and learned from. I have always wanted to
share what the finance industry knows.

For the everyday person to access how it works,
how they can participate, and how to understand and
trust underpinning systems like superannuation is a real
passion of mine. Everybody deserves the chance to learn
and be part of something much more strategic, profitable,

and sustainable for the future, and this industry is all about that. Now, you might be rolling your eyes and thinking I'm a fangirl, but the reality is, over the years, having made multiple TV shows, podcasts, books, and online learning resources around money, I've seen the transformation in people when something resonates and they understand how to apply their learned wisdom to their own lives. This is my buzz. Your financial flashpoints are my thing. That's my passion, and a big part of my purpose. At times it drives me crazy, because it's a path that means I stay independent, run my own show, and take on everything that comes with that. But it is the job I'm here to do, and I have known that for a long time.

So what's your thing? What are you passionate about? What do you believe you are good at? Forget what you have been told in your past. That was then, and this is now. Of course, there is a lot of self-work that has to go on here – and I would recommend talking to someone if you find it hard to get past. At the very least, you owe it to yourself to explore your options.

ANTICIPATING MONEY PITFALLS

The Dark Side of Money

Like all things in life, money has a difficult dark side. When it comes to money, we can't deny the emotions we attach to it. Money and emotions go hand in hand. Every single one of us holds deep emotional connections to money: shame, pride, guilt, embarrassment, jealousy, blame, envy, and resentment, just to name a few. It's also possible to feel happiness, joy, and freedom toward money. But when you don't have control of your money situation, negative emotions will creep up and add to your stress levels.

Jane and her mum, sitting around her kitchen table. There are bills laying around them. Stressed, awkward air.

JANE   **I can't believe how the electricity bill has gone up! It's well over two hundred dollars more than the last one!**

JANE'S MUM   Yes, the cost of living just keeps rising. Your father and I worry about you and the girls all the time.

JANE   **No need to worry, Mum. We are fine. And you and Dad help a lot. I am fine.**

JANE'S MUM   All three of these bills are due in May. How are you going to pay them all?

JANE   **I guess I'll have to chase Nick for child support again. God, he is just the worst. I am so sick of him not living up to his end of the divorce.**

JANE'S MUM   It is certainly no surprise to me. You know what I think of that man.

JANE   **All too well, Mother. I have heard it a thousand times. I picked the worst possible choice of a man to be the girls' father.**

JANE'S MUM   I don't want to fight. You do an amazing job with those girls, and we adore them and you.

JANE   **I know, Mum. I'm just so tired of juggling everything. I am never enough. At work, with the girls, with the bills. I am just so gutted that my life is this way.**

JANE'S MUM   You are educated and remarkable. It is not over yet. Things can change.

JANE   **I don't see how.**

It's easy to lose perspective when we're racing through life. How do you feel when a bill comes in? Jane is overwhelmed by bills and disappointment in her life. The act of thinking about how to pay for everything has her reflecting on her failed relationship and where else she sees herself failing. This spiral of negative thinking does not give Jane opportunities to find a way to change her situation. Instead, she is stuck on the man who let her down more than once and keeping up a brave face to her parents, who she knows worry about her constantly. That just makes her feel guilty.

While Jane's mum has always been beyond supportive, she is not really helpful when it comes to teaching her daughter new ways she can change her situation. She simply doesn't know, so she shows up and does what she knows best: cooks and cleans and feeds the kids. And Josie is very grateful for that. Her parents being hands-on was a godsend. But their baby boomer views on life, kids, and marriage make it hard to hide how disappointed they are, for their precious daughter and the results of her life choices. This makes Jane's heart ache.

I've learned that there's no point in negative self-talk because of the choices you've made and the unhealthy habits you (and a lot of us) have formed. There's also no point in pointing the finger and blaming our parents, our partners, or even our kids for where we're at with our money situation. This leads to us feeling shame, resentment, embarrassment, and guilt around money and gets us nowhere.

Sometimes it takes talking with someone different about your life to help spark a financial flashpoint for you. It was that way with Jane. But it also takes us behaving differently, not just for everyone else, but ourselves. We need to reprogram ourselves to not jump to the negative first. This means surrounding your suggestive brain with positive intentions.

I have found, if you want to start thinking positively about money, start talking positively about it. Stick notes up on the wall, put reminders in your phone, write them on your arm – whatever works for you. Ask yourself, *What do I want to feel about money, in an ideal world?* Write it down and post it on the wall and around the house, so you can remind yourself every day. I like mantras like, "I'm in control of my money situation," and "Money is coming to me."

Turning the negatives into positives will train your brain over time to feel good about money, which will help you attract more positive pathways to your solutions.

The people you spend your time with and what they say about money also matters. If the people around you have a positive or negative relationship with money, chances are it will rub off on you. If you want a positive relationship with money, you need to examine your inner monologue about money as well as what's happening externally around you. Take note. Is what those around you are saying about money positive or negative?

ADOPTING A PURPOSEFUL PERSPECTIVE AROUND MONEY

Can Money Make You Happy?
They say money can't buy happiness, but money problems are a big reason why people are living stuck in a cycle that seems to be going nowhere. Money really does impact our lives in a dramatic way, for better or worse. It can give you lots of joy and freedom, or it can be a source of suffering if you let it.

We see our characters looking around the group contentedly, after their spas—in white robes, champagne in hand. They are at the luxury resort at the Blue Mountains that Brad's EA booked.

BRAD
THINKING TO HIMSELF

I have to be in three time zones next week. It's a crazy life. I love it, and I'm grateful for it, but there's not much outside of work for me. I'm so glad I can afford to shout the whole gang away for our annual blowout. It means the world to me.

RUSS

I am so grateful to have time away from the grind. I feel genuinely happy, for real.

KAREN

God, the food here is phenomenal, and no cooking for me! With the comfort level of this robe, I'm in heaven.

JOSIE

This wine is perfect. I feel 100 percent relaxed. Brad is looking fine.

JASPER

The unlimited bar is top shelf. Wow. That fire is perfect. And I think I might get lucky tonight.

JANE

Did he just say that? I think he did. And he might be right. God, sex. Romance. Friends. Yay.

This trip with friends happened because one of them was a billionaire. But note, even in this scenario, the one most financially successful by a long shot, Brad, was the one who was grateful for being able to give. His money allowed his friends to experience luxuries they would not otherwise be exposed to. Of course he enjoyed it, but with his level of responsibility in business, his mind was pretty much on it twenty-four seven. There was little respite.

Getting happiness from money is individual and personal. No one can tell you what's going to make you happy except you. And only you know how much you're going to need to make your dreams come true.

If Only Things Were Different
To get anywhere with this book (and, quite frankly, in life), you must be willing to get really honest with yourself about where you are in life, what you genuinely want, what you really want to change, and how you want to be remembered.

It's okay if you don't know where to start. But I do suggest dreaming big and thinking outside the box. See that there is another way forward for you, especially if you've been limiting yourself for quite some time.

Start wondering from an "if only" perspective. *If only*...I could have that dream house or the money to travel, quit my job and work for myself, be able to start a family or a business, or have enough while being able to donate to others. We might catch ourselves saying, "If only things were different..." Well, what if things could be different? Let yourself go there. It's a good way to figure out what you truly want. *If only* you had the money or time or freedom to do what you really wanted to do: What would you do? What would that different life really look like? How would it make you feel?

The honest answers to these questions can only come from a place of being authentic with yourself and clear on your own values. What do you truly value in life? (Not just things you say you value, but don't align your behaviours and decisions with.) What's more important to you than anything else? Is it your health? Your home?

Your freedom? Providing for your kids? The greater good of humanity? The ability to be freely creative in your job? What about the ability to travel where and when you want (forgetting certain travel restrictions for a moment)? It's only by looking at these questions that you start to see what it is you truly want in life.

Usually "if only" starts with not yet knowing the actions to take to make our dreams a reality. They are nice thoughts or aspirations we hide away and think about when nobody else is around.

Most people have made up their minds that they will always work at a job, never make a lot of money, and must do this for the next few decades until they retire. But what if it was different?

Without long-term clarity, we go from thing to thing, job to job, and holiday to holiday, with no clear intention or goal.

Rethink What Success Means
In the decades I have worked in and around the money industry, I have made countless observations about people who have money. How they act, how they speak, even how they dress. And while there are many things that are different about all these people, there are two common denominators that come up time and time again.

What I have observed is, the more money you have, the less you tend to think about it. The billionaires I've come across are the opposite of frivolous with money. Most of the time they don't even talk about it or make a point of showing it off. A lot of wealthy people still drive older cars and shop for bargains. Most of them don't waste money. In fact, they are far more likely to be frugal. Why? Because their money fuels a bigger cause for them: their passion. Whether that passion is philanthropy (which is increasingly common for people with a high net worth) or investing (which naturally creates wealth), billionaires pursue their passions relentlessly.

So how can we learn from these two factors – values and passion – to improve our money situation? We're becoming more and more aware that there is no point in doing a job just for money, not in the long term at least.

Our work accounts for far too much of our life to spend it doing something we don't care about.

Ask yourself, what matters more to you than anything else? It might not be a new car after all. Or owning a house over renting. Or maybe it is. This is your life and your dream, so it can be whatever you want it to be. For some, it could be the freedom to travel and work from anywhere, while for others it could be building a dream home to raise a family for life.

My views on success have changed wildly as I've gotten older. I have learned that your intuition usually tells you when it's time for a change. The seasons of my life have moved with the passing of time, kids arriving and getting older, and work leading me to know what I don't want to do as much as what I do.

It seems in order to get what you really want in life, you have to know what it is you want. Spend some time thinking about who and what is important to you.

YOU	**What really makes me happy?**
ALSO YOU	Chocolate
YOU	**Obviously. But bigger picture.**
ALSO YOU	Time with family.
YOU	**Okay, that's true. But with work and the commute, you really only do that on weekends.**
ALSO YOU	So your work and commute are preventing you from doing what you really love?
YOU	**Well, yes. But we need the money.**
ALSO YOU	Yes, we do. How much? Maybe time to do a new budget on that free website to see where we are at. I've lost track.
YOU	**Sounds boring, but okay. But can we think of ways we can change the work/commute situation?**
ALSO YOU	Maybe we can. Let's see how much we need to make some changes.

Reinventing Your Money Story

It is possible to set yourself free to live the life you really want at any age. It doesn't matter if you're in your twenties, thirties, forties, fifties, sixties, seventies, or beyond. There is never a bad time to start living the life you want.

> **YOU**   Well, nothing can change for me. I'm too old to do anything else.
>
> **ALSO YOU**   Not that I have actually tried to do anything else. I guess I could take a look at what's around.
>
> **YOU**   I have always loved the thought of being a counsellor and helping people in hard times.
>
> **ALSO YOU**   I saw an article about people training to do that a few months back.
>
> **YOU**   I might google that, it can't hurt. Wow, turns out I found a twelve-month, part-time, online program.
>
> **ALSO YOU**   Gee, maybe I could sign up for that. Unreal to think that, in a year, I'd be doing something completely different. I can study on top of my existing work for that long.
>
> **YOU**   Something to look forward to. What else could I change?
>
> **ALSO YOU**   Hmmm, one step at a time.

Reinventing your money story will set you free to live the life you really want at any age.

The Ten-Year Plan
I like to look at what things will look like in ten years' time because there's a lot you can achieve in ten years. But many of us don't give ourselves the patience, perseverance, or time it takes to achieve our goals. Rarely, if ever, do they just happen overnight. Having

a plan that goes beyond what your life looks like now and instead looks few years ahead will really boost your chances of getting there.

While I haven't always been someone who can plan twenty years out, the older I get, the easier this has become.

Opens on a BBQ scene in Russ and Karen's backyard. The kids are on their phones.

RUSS

I can't see myself in accounting forever. The client load is killing me.

KAREN

Well, it's not like you have to put it up with it forever.

RUSS

Well, we have six more years of school fees, so it sure isn't looking short-term.

KAREN

You always wanted to be a lecturer or teacher. Maybe you should look into that. We only will need one set of school fees in three years – the others will have graduated.

RUSS

You are right, I did always fancy myself an academic.

KAREN

Let's find out what they pay. Maybe it's possible we could make a change.

RUSS

Wow. In ten years, we could be living near a uni campus. You with your own business. Me a lecturer.

KAREN

Ha! Imagine that. Sounds cool.

RUSS

Doesn't it.

Russ didn't think about what he wanted when their conversation started. He started with what he didn't want: the continuing workload and stress of his current job. But it was Karen who was able to point him in the right direction as far as mindset.

> # LONG-TERM THINKING NEEDS TO BE MOTIVATING WHEN IT COMES TO CHANGING YOUR LIFE AND MONEY. WHO DO YOU WANT TO BE AND WHAT WOULD IT COST?

YOUR LIFE TEN YEARS FROM NOW

Imagine your life in five years, ten years, and twenty years. What does it look like at each interval? What do you see yourself doing at each of these stages? What is your family like? What experiences do you want to have achieved in each of these periods?

Get a pen and paper out and write a list with one page for each of those stages in your life. You can write a letter to yourself of what your life looks like in the future. Put in as much detail as you can. Write it as if it was happening now. How old are you? What are you doing? Where are you living? What's your job? What are your hobbies? Who are you spending time with? Describe the experiences, even the details of the holidays you want to take, so that you can start to imagine them happening and they start to feel real.

$\longrightarrow$

Start to get an understanding of how your major expenses could shift over time. Will your kids be out of school or out of the house by then? Will you potentially get an inheritance? This will help you focus on the bigger plan and the fact that you can build a financial plan that shifts as your life shifts.

Give yourself a chance to visualise the life you really want. You won't believe the power of actually putting on paper the dreams you have for your life and your family.

Air Out the Dirty Laundry

Once you have an idea of what you want your dream life to look like, it's time to look at all the things that have been holding you back from creating that. There's a gap that exists between creating your ideal life and the life you're currently living.

Wherever you are, there is bound to be something that you've been putting off, ignoring, or avoiding, or something that's been niggling at you that you know you should probably address but haven't.

Start creating a laundry list of all the barriers that are stopping you from living that ideal life. Recognise what they are and acknowledge the dirty laundry that's been hanging around for some time. It could be a lack of time, a job you've been hanging onto, or something else entirely.

Take everything into account. Exactly how much debt do you have? What are all your monthly repayments? Only then you can do a true assessment of your financial situation. Many of us don't know the true figure, and we often forget to consider bills that arrive quarterly and things that are bought annually, like presents.

This isn't about being hard on yourself. You can leave the criticism at the door. It's about recognising the good, the bad, and the ugly, and seeing what needs to shift, but doing it with compassion. This is not a place for resentment or blame or being annoyed at yourself or anyone else.

Consider what changes you could make to make things easier on your bank account. Could you cancel some subscriptions? Get a better deal on your mobile plan? Change health insurers? I have found that all the little things add up, and getting your monthly overheads down is the first step to an easier life.

What things are keeping you stuck and stopping you from making changes? What's in your way? Is it debt, family commitments, aging parents, young kids at home, a lack of education, not having the right degree, a lack of experience or knowledge, not having family or partner support, a lack of savings, your health or an illness, a tragedy you haven't been able to overcome, or a lack of belief in yourself?

Write it all down, even the ugly bits you don't really want to face and the things that seem impossible to confront – especially those bits.

What could you do to ease the pressure? Can you live somewhere less expensive? Could you downgrade your car or take public transport? Whatever the decisions, at least you have the power to make them and lower your stress by being informed and proactive, instead of just worrying.

Facing Uncertainty and Fear

One thing the COVID-19 pandemic has taught us as a collective is that there is no certainty in life. We really don't know what tomorrow will bring. I know this can induce anxiety, but we need to get comfortable with the discomfort of not knowing what's around the corner. All you can do is plan for the best-case scenario while considering the worst-case too, and leave a little room for life to flow because some things are out of your hands.

Opens with Brad at an airfield, about to board a plane. He is talking on his phone.

BRAD Rach, we need that client function to happen. The team won't have their sales quotas without that event to close deals.

EA RACHEL I'm sorry, Brad. There's been a COVID outbreak at the hotel, and half the guests have been exposed. It's not going to happen.

BRAD Thank god we have cash reserves. There's been so many cancellations this year. It pays to be prepared.

EA RACHEL Yes. So many of our suppliers have gone out of business. It's getting quite scary.

While not everyone is as lucky as Brad when it comes to access to capital, the reality is that all of us need to be prepared for the unexpected. Having access to cash is critical for giving yourself peace of mind that, no matter what happens, you and your family will get through. In this world, cash is king. Make sure you have a buffer in your own life. Make building it a priority, no matter where you are now. Three to six months of living expenses is a great place to start.

Facing Your Debts

Debt is building up more each year, and the statistics are honestly quite frightening. All across the world, we are racking up debt faster than we are producing. In other words, we are spending way more than we earn.

If you are leveraged with a business, have run up credit cards, or have taken out a personal loan, you might be feeling the pressure of making ends meet.

> *Scene starts with Josie in her office, sitting with her financial controller at work.*
>
> JOSIE   My god, that Amex bill keeps going up. Use the Mastercard to pay the suppliers this month.
>
> FC   Okay. There's already $10,000 on there from the event we just paid for.
>
> JOSIE   Okay, just make it work. We can pay them off next month when the invoices get paid.
>
> FC   I will get on it. It would be great if you could find another $25,000 in billings this month. We have had a lot of costs.
>
> JOSIE   Yes, I hear you. *(Sighs)* I will go get my black book out and look at who could be a sale.

Josie runs a business that is successful by anyone's standards. But it is extremely dependent on her to make sales. Juggling credit cards and costs in the business is all part of the reason her stress levels keep going up. While she may have clients paying money, her costs are also large. It's a never-ending hamster wheel to keep it all going. It is only when Josie gets advice that she starts to think about taking some risk away by selling part of her business to key staff. That way all the responsibility is not on her.

How much debt have you accumulated? How much interest are you paying on your loans and credit cards? How often do you rely on your credit cards? Do you pay your credit cards on time? How can you start paying down the debt?

Debt plays a huge role in the stress of keeping your head above water. The pressures debt can bring to your life can be debilitating. Being stuck in a situation of debt can be truly devastating and difficult to face when you're there. But there is a way to get out of it.

> MANY PEOPLE START WITH THE SMALLEST DEBTS FIRST, AND WORK THEIR WAY THROUGH THE LIST. OTHERS CONSOLIDATE SMALLER DEBTS INTO A BIGGER ONE AND FOCUS ON THAT. WHATEVER METHOD YOU CHOOSE, MAKE SURE THE HIGHER-INTEREST ITEMS ARE THE ONES YOU ARE TACKLING MORE URGENTLY. THEY ARE WHAT IS COSTING YOU MORE.

Control Your Spending and Save More
There's no two ways about it. You've got to commit to a savings plan and pay down any personal debt you have to get ahead.

Spending without a plan doesn't seem to cost that much at the time. But when you look back, you'll see it was the opportunity cost that was the real price tag. If you had put that money you spent into something that increased in value, what would it be worth now? If you had spent that time on a project that was successful, how much profit could have been made? Question the long-term value of whatever you buy from here on.

Ask yourself if what you're spending your money on is genuinely contributing to your happiness. If it's not, try taking a break from those expenses. Research shows that we can be happy if we spend more on things like experiences, buying back our time by delegating tasks, and investing in ourselves and others.

It's about distribution of your income. How can you better distribute it to the things that make you happy? Can you cut down on the daily coffee to give yourself a spare hundred dollars a month? You might even decide to put that extra money into savings and buy yourself something even better in a few months or a year or put it into an investment fund that will grow over time.

Having a little bit of extra cash in your savings account, even five hundred dollars a month, can significantly put you at ease and make you feel more in control overall. So, if that's the case, how can you keep more cash in your hand? What can you cut back on to have this extra money in your account each month?

How much do you really need to be saving? What are you saving for? What do you spend the bulk of your money on? Is what you're spending your money on making you happy or miserable? What do you want to spend your money on? Asking yourself these questions is so valuable to get on the path of making money work for you!

> **MAKE A PROMISE TO YOURSELF THAT YOU'RE NOT GOING TO STEAL FROM FUTURE YOU ANYMORE.**

Short-Term Sacrifices and Long-Term Gains

Saving money is often associated with sacrifice, but what happens if you start to associate money with freedom? The money you save, and don't spend on unnecessary things that don't make you happy, gives you more freedom for the future.

The best way to stick to a good money habit is to automate it. Make it as easy as possible for yourself by automating your savings from your wage, payments into your retirement fund, and mortgage repayments.

Automations are single actions that set your future habits on autopilot, so you don't have to think about them. They simply become automatic.

A little bit of time upfront can set you up for a long-term outcome that will reap rewards. Automate as much as possible in your life so you can set and forget and never think about it again, except maybe once or twice a year when you do your tax or review your overall finances. You can even automate a reminder in your calendar to make sure you do your taxes on time and do your financial review.

The more you can automate to set and forget, the less stressed you'll be about money and the more in control you'll feel.

Know what you need as your basic amount to cover all your expenses, and automate all your regular payments. Once you know all the basics are paid, the rest is fun money – woohoo! – but first you need to know what your baseline is. This might change from month to month, but if you know your baseline, you'll be covered for the basics every month. And that means stress-free living and more cash for fun.

> **AUTOMATION IS THE ULTIMATE WAY TO LOCK IN A FUTURE BEHAVIOUR, RATHER THAN RELYING ON WILLPOWER AND REMEMBERING.**

What can you automate today? Think about putting away a set amount each month into your retirement plan, your savings account for a holiday, your emergency fund, and some extra cash for fun.

Why You Need to Look at Your Retirement Plan Now
It is never too early to start looking at the money you're going to retire with. The sooner the better, because the more money you invest earlier, the more compound interest will accumulate, and the sooner you'll be able to retire. Retirement savings are the ultimate Plan B, and it is highly likely that most of us will need it.

Retirement doesn't mean you have to stop working. It means you can be financially stable enough to not work. It is a choice. But research shows most people are nowhere near what they need to have in retirement savings. Even a million dollars in your retirement fund won't get you the leisurely retirement you're imagining.

The first thing is to check how much you have in your retirement savings. Do you know where it all is, and how much is in there? Is it split over several accounts, or is it consolidated in one place? What retirement fund are you with? Have you thought about comparing or switching?

Do you know how much you need to retire comfortably? How much are you putting away each month? Each year? If you have a partner, do you know how much he or she has compared to you? If you work for yourself, have you been paying your future self?

These are all important questions you need to be asking yourself.

> **WHEN WE ARE YOUNG, WE THINK RETIREMENT IS FAR AWAY...BUT TIME PASSES. THE EARLIER YOU START WITH RETIREMENT SAVINGS, THE BETTER OFF YOU'LL BE.**

Don't Discount Your Health

Without your health, money means nothing. If you get sick, you'll be spending a lot of time, energy, and money on getting better, so you're better off investing in your health now. We all know that health is more important than money, yet many of us choose work and making money instead of looking after our health and well-being.

It's important to confront all aspects of your health and well-being. How much are you spending on your health? Do you need to invest more into looking after your health, with things like yoga or a gym membership? Do you have health insurance to protect yourself if anything goes wrong? Are you spending money on cigarettes and alcohol that's draining not only your wallet but your health too? Something else that contributes to our health (it's not just exercise and food!) is who we spend our time with. Who do you hang out with? Do they lift you up or drain you?

Stress is another reason our health suffers. Of course, money can be a cause of our stress, but so can our relationships and our responsibilities. I've found that when people aren't really living the life they want, they tend to get sick. Do what you can to put your health first and think about how money can help you get there.

You might also ask yourself some questions like: Are you spending money on others when you don't need to be, and is this causing stress in your life? Who do you need to lean on more? Who are you allowing to rely on you too much? Does anything need to change in your relationships? Have you been avoiding talking with your partner about anything? Have you been honest with those closest to you? Is avoidance causing you stress?

Do you have health insurance, life insurance, and income protection? Do you need to get it or reassess what you have? What would happen if you or someone in your family got sick, too sick to work, or worse? The way to protect yourself and your family against this is to determine the right kind of insurance to meet your long-term needs.

Life insurance is hard to understand, expensive, and just plain boring to organise, but having the worst happen without it would create deep long-term pain. It is worth looking into or at least adding it to your list of things to do. There are different kinds of insurance, designed for different things. Life is one thing, and TPD (Total and Permanent Disablement) is another. I would always recommend talking with a qualified adviser about the best insurance for you.

Just don't wait too long to get around to it. The older you are, the harder it is to get insurance, as more things go wrong with you physically.

Have you thought about making a will, even if you're young? What about estate planning if you own a property? If you have any assets, have you planned out where they will go if something should happen to you? If you do have any assets, this is something you need to sort out. We never know what is around the corner. We tend to put things like this off, but it's best to just get it done.

USE YOUR YEARS WISELY. YOU CANNOT GET THEM BACK.

Leaning into Delayed Satisfaction

Having a good balance with money is about valuing delayed satisfaction (having money when you retire or for the things you truly desire) over instant gratification from the temptation of having what you want now (spending money you could otherwise save).

The best way is to figure out how much you need, automate your savings (including retirement money and investments), and allocate spending money for the things you truly enjoy (like weekend trips away and takeout for dinner on Fridays).

Many choices you make will not benefit you immediately. And because we don't see the results immediately, we tend to give up too quickly. You need patience and persistence with any plan. Do your research, figure out what you need, and implement it. Then, let it do its thing.

We tend to value the present more than the future – until we get there and realise we have a problem because we didn't think about our future selves before.

Instant gratification is what gets us in trouble. It might feel good to get a new pair of shoes, but in a few weeks or months, when they're old and worn, you won't appreciate them anymore. Putting that hundred dollars into savings where it can accumulate interest is something your future self will thank you for. You'll have a hundred dollars plus interest, instead of an old pair of shoes.

> ANYTHING THAT BEGINS WITH "F*** IT, LIFE'S SHORT," IS PROBABLY NOT GOOD FOR YOUR FUTURE SELF AND YOUR LONG-TERM PLANS.

We all need more than one account. A separate account for wish-list things like holidays, and a longer-term account that is all about your longer-term goals for the future, like a house. This could be a higher-interest savings account, or a low-cost index fund, depending on when you need the money.

And then your retirement savings is another thing again. Download the app on your phone for this as well, and move money in there whenever you have a windfall with no plan attached to it. With automation and separate accounts, you will start to find your life becoming easier and more aligned to the goals you have for the future.

Seeing fifty dollars hit your savings account for something you really want – like a holiday or a house – can give the same immediate pleasure that buying something would have given you. Sticking to habits like this is only possible when it feels good.

> ## ONE OF THE MOST SATISFYING FEELINGS IS THE FEELING OF PROGRESS. SO PERSIST, BE PATIENT, AND KEEP GOING.

When you make a plan, you are actually making decisions for your future self. It is important to focus on the long-term benefits to see the value in taking the steps and putting the work in now. Any decision and action should align with your long-term goals.

Most of us delay action because we are avoiding pain. It will take a little bit of sacrifice up front, but after a while, you won't even notice it. Nothing happens when you don't buy that pair of shoes, but you will feel good knowing that money has gone into savings for something even bigger and better in your future, such as your dream home or the travelling you're going to do, or a new wardrobe that you're going to buy once a year instead of making impulse purchases whenever you feel like it.

In those moments of temptation, really weigh whether it's worth it. Sometimes it is (like a last-minute trip to see family or a spontaneous dinner) but most of the time, we spend money in the moment when we don't really need to. Think twice before you do. Just ask yourself if your future self will thank you for it or have regrets.

I made some money mistakes in my twenties and thirties because I wanted to spend money and treat myself to new things I hadn't had before. I saw people driving around in fancy cars and I wanted that too. The fast cars, the nice clothes, the fine dining, the big house.

But eventually, I learned the hard way that those aren't the things that make you happy – especially if you end up racking up debt to get them, which leads to nothing but stress – and financial stress is the worst. You end up losing money on things like cars and clothes. Unless they're things you truly love and look after for a long time, and they're things you can truly afford, you are making your life harder.

All those clothes I bought in my twenties that I wore once or twice, I regret, and the things I put on credit really weren't worth the stress of paying them off. Freedom is not getting into debt and spending on whatever you want. It's about financial freedom, which gives you time and autonomy to do what you want with your life and the ability to spend your money on the things you love without needing to use a credit card. That's the ultimate freedom.

FREEDOM IS THE ULTIMATE FINANCIAL REWARD.

Think about the Bigger Picture

Remember your ten-year plan, when you asked yourself what you really want out of your life? Don't forget that you're doing all of this so you can spend time and money doing what's important to you, spending them on the things that are going to bring you happiness.

What does the bigger picture look like for you? What do you really want in life? What is the state of your cash flow and debt, and is there anything you need to take control of here so you can move in the direction you really want to go? What are your spending habits in relation to your income and savings? Have you got the important things in place, like retirement savings and life insurance? How are you prioritising your health and yourself?

What changes can you make? How can you relieve the pressure? There are a few levers you can pull in your financial life, but the two biggest to change your situation are these: How can you lower your overheads? And how can you bring more money in?

Opens on Karen and Russ sitting at the dining table after dinner with the kids.

KAREN
Okay, I have been going through our monthly expenses, and I think I found a few ways to save a bit of money. This is going to help us take those holidays we all want.

RUSS
Holidays? Great. What are they clever, lady?

KAREN
Well, for a start, we don't need the Foxtel subscription. It's expensive and really only has sport on it.

RUSS
But I watch the sport! I don't want to lose that.

KAREN
But it's forty dollars we could be putting in the holiday account each month.

$\longrightarrow$

RUSS *GRUMBLING*	Well, okay, I guess so.
KAREN	I am also cancelling my gym membership. I have found a group of walkers who I am going to join instead. So that's another fifty dollars a month we save.
KIDS	We don't need the Disney channel either, Mum. Let's just keep Netflix. That's twenty dollars.
KAREN	Great. We now have another $110 a month going into our holiday funds. Well done, family.

There is not one answer to each of these questions about saving – there are hundreds of answers. As you can see by the script, the answers are different for each person. And they may involve you making decisions that are initially tough. They also might affect others in your family. But at the end of the day, you must make decisions that protect yourself, your energy, and your joy. Because they are things that look after everyone else in turn.

Taking Action Is the Only Way Forward
The thing with action is you've just got to do it. It's like ripping off a Band-Aid. There's no easy way around it other than just doing it. Otherwise, what you want just becomes a pipe dream. It becomes an intention with no real plan.

Our tendency to "deal with things later" means we don't actually get what we want. This leads to a lifetime of "settling," rather than using the years we have been given to set ourselves up to our best advantage. To get what we want, we need to unlearn this lack of focus, and create some real, tangible action.

But we humans resist things that feel hard, unfamiliar, or out of our comfort zone. We go back to what feels comfortable, time and time again. That's why it's so hard to stick to a diet or New Year's resolutions. If it were easy, we'd all be smashing our goals and living our best lives with rock-solid abs – but it isn't as simple as that. We are human, and it is human nature to resist what's hard and seek comfort and ease instead. It's why we order a pizza instead of cooking the veggies we have in the fridge.

It's about comfort over discomfort. We also tend to take the easy route when we feel a little uncertain about our abilities. A tiny bit of self-doubt can stop us from doing the thing we know we need to. Setting up the savings account and automating payments, consolidating our retirement savings, starting to pay down debt, learning to invest our money, stopping ourselves from spending so much, and calling the tax accountant: they're not hard to do, but we resist what feels slightly uncomfortable and unfamiliar – or even just plain boring.

> THE BEST WAY IS TO JUST DO IT. JUST START. TAKING ACTION OVERRIDES ANY ANXIETY OR FEAR YOU MIGHT FEEL.

MOVING TOWARD MONEY MILESTONES

Starting to believe in yourself and where your life can lead is the first step. It's not all going to happen at once, but every small step you take, every little win, is getting you closer to the new life you want to live – much closer than if you hadn't put some thought and action into it at all.

By imagining what you want, and addressing what's holding you back and blocking you, you've already made some traction. When you put some actions in place to start addressing these blocks, you can start to see changes happen.

Confronting the costs involved and getting creative with how you can supplement that – with a side gig or just selling some things around the house you no longer need – can really get the wheels rolling.

Persistence is key, and being open about your challenges with yourself and with others will help you stay on track. You can't do this completely alone. Find someone you can rely on to help you get there.

Most of all, stay focused on the big picture. Imagine what you want and never give up.

Nothing happens overnight, but you'll be glad you took these steps today when you look back in a few months or years. Before you know it, you'll start seeing these changes play out – and there's no better feeling than seeing the fruits of your labour, as you start living the life you want to be living.

Woohoo! You've made it through the most important chapter of this book! You've asked yourself some serious questions throughout this chapter, but here are a few more to reflect on. They are all designed to remind you what really matters. From there, you can figure out what money is needed to make it work.

HOW DO YOU WANT TO BE REMEMBERED?

WHAT IS MOST IMPORTANT TO YOU?

WITH UNLIMITED MONEY, WHO WOULD YOU GIVE TO?

HAVE A COURAGEOUS CONVERSATION WITH YOURSELF

Pour yourself some wine, get some snacks, or even take yourself out for a meal (or order takeout). You could even do this while soaking in the bath where no one can interrupt you, while listening to your favourite tunes. This is a time for some real "me time." You're going to get much more out of this than watching something on Netflix.

You could get out a pen and a notepad or a big piece of paper, or open a blank document on your computer so you can write some notes. It's time to have a little conversation with yourself.

Let's start with facing your beliefs about money...

- What do you need to unlearn about money? (You can find a free tool on my website to help you diagnose this.)

- What did your parents say about money that became part of your beliefs too?

- What do you keep telling yourself that makes you feel like you're not good with money?

- Think about who you're spending time with: in the workplace, your social circles, and your family members. What are their beliefs about money, and how is it rubbing off on you?

- What new beliefs about money can you pick up?

- What can you tell yourself about money that's positive, even if you don't quite believe it yet?

Now, imagine your dream life...

- Imagine your biggest, boldest life...what does that look like?

- What's your dream life, if money weren't really an obstacle?

- What do you really want in life, deep down?

- If you could click your fingers and have whatever you wanted, what would it be?

- What potential do you see for yourself?

- What does your ideal life look like in ten years?

- If only...you could really live your dream life, what would that look like? Allow yourself to go there and *dream big.*

What's holding you back from the dream?

- What do you want to change in your life, and what's in your way or holding you back?

- Do you need to create some boundaries, such as with your kids, your parents, or your partner, to allow yourself to live a truer life that's going to benefit you?

- What are you too scared to spend money on?

- When you think about what you really want from life, what could you change to get it?

Let's find your "why"...

- What do you care about more than anything?

- What would you invest your money in, or spend your money on, if you had it?

- What are your top five core values? Your health, furthering your education, investing in your freedom, your relationships, your kids, where you live, security, following your passions, travelling, or allowing yourself to do the job you really want to do?

- What are you spending money on that is making you happy, and what are you spending money on that isn't adding to your happiness?

Facing the reality...

- Do you know what your baseline is for all your monthly and annual expenses?

- Have you got debt you need to face? How much?

- How can you start paying off your debt and stop the habit of accumulating it?

- Think about what you're spending money on, beyond the basics, and why.

- Do you need to start writing down what you're spending money on?

- How much do you really spend on things that don't actually add much value to your life?

- What's the one thing you're spending too much money on?

Setting yourself up...

- Can you start automating payments into your savings account?

- What about your retirement fund? Do you know how much is in there and how much you need to retire comfortably?

- Have you got life insurance? What about a will?

- How can you create a savings plan and get to know your cash flow?

ON MY WEBSITE I HAVE SOME FREE RESOURCES TO START THE JOURNEY. THERE ARE ALSO DEDICATED COURSES THAT CAN HELP YOU STRUCTURE A PLAN FOR LIVING THE LIFE YOU WANT.

Chapter 2

THE EYE-OPENING + CONFRONTING CONVERSATION YOU NEED TO HAVE WITH YOUR PARTNER

2

MONEY
MATRIMONY

On a scale of one to ten, how honest are you with your partner when it comes to money?

Come on, come clean.

If you've lied to your partner about money – sneaky credit card use, being deceptive about how much you paid for something, buying shoes or stocks without telling, secretly slipping some extra cash to the kids when you said you wouldn't – you aren't alone.

Look, we've all scuffed up a pair of new shoes and told our partner they're old (or maybe that's just me, but hey, I learned this behaviour from someone!).

Maybe you've done something bigger, like gambled the savings away or put money into an investment that went bust. Maybe that money you've both been putting away for your kids' education has been funding a little side project for some time now.

I have friends who've been victims of systematic lies where their partner has racked up a lot of debt and taken out a secret second mortgage – I mean, that's serious stuff. But I've seen it happen.

Transparent Talks about Money

Lying to a partner about money is more common than you might think. Research shows that anywhere from a third to almost half of us admit to having lied to our partners.

Lying is human nature, and we do it for several reasons – to protect ourselves and to try not to hurt the people around us. Maybe we do it to avoid conflict and keep the peace and avoid disappointments. Maybe we just know our partner wouldn't agree, so we do it anyway and avoid having the conversation about it.

Most of us could probably be a little more honest with our partners when it comes to money. And it's important for several reasons.

You probably don't need me to tell you that money is one of the leading causes of separation and divorce.

It's something couples argue about all the time, no matter how much each partner is earning, and financial stress that builds over time can be catastrophic in a relationship. Whether you have a lot of money (individually or combined) or not, money can cause major rifts in relationships.

Being Financially Honest with Your Partner

Do you feel you need to sit down with your partner to discuss some bigger things you've been putting off? When was the last time you sat down and really opened up to your partner about something you've been avoiding – something that's been giving you grief and you haven't told them yet?

Maybe you don't want them to go out drinking on the weekend, or you think it would help you both save more for a house if they didn't order from Uber Eats so much. Maybe you've seen the hidden shopping bags or found out the credit card was over the limit again.

Opens on Jane and Jasper having wine in the lounge room of her house.

JANE   I love this wine. Who made it again?

JASPER   Friends of mine who own a vineyard.

JANE   Cool, how much is it a bottle?

JASPER   I am not sure; I buy it by the case.

JANE   Case? That's a lot of wine! What does that cost?

$\longrightarrow$

JASPER	Not much. Practically a freebie. *Knowing he spent $180 on that case.*
JANE	Oh, okay. That's good. I can take a bottle over to Mum and Dad then.
JASPER	Ah, sure, no problem. *(Awkward silence.)*

Jasper didn't want Jane to think he spent too much on booze. He was hoping to make a good impression, and did not want how much he spent on alcohol to be an issue. This is only going to be obvious later in their relationship, as Jane realises how much Jasper does spend on drinking.

If we're going to live together, share our lives, and maybe raise children together, we've got to be honest with each other. A good relationship starts with trust and honesty, and it all comes down to clear communication. The healthiest, happiest (and wealthiest) couples don't hesitate to talk about their finances, even if it's a bit uncomfortable at times. The more you do it, the easier it will become. You've just got to get comfortable with being uncomfortable to start the conversation.

We have a long way to go to get past the shame and social stigma when talking about money with our partners, no matter how long we've been together.

It's easy for me to say you've got to be open and transparent with your partner about your finances. If that is not how you have done things before, then it might take some setting up for that first conversation. If you are in a new relationship, it is easy to watch for the signs on money. Are they spending on credit cards? Do they seem stressed about money? Or ultra-tight? The signs of money personality and situation are clearly there from the beginning.

When you are in a relationship, sometimes approaching a topic like money is all about timing. Don't bring up money when your partner is stressed or focused on something else. Set a time. Make a date. Yes, bring wine, or chocolate, or any other conversational lubricant that will help this go smoothly.

Because this isn't the conversation you have where you pull out the credit card statement and ask about the line items. This is much bigger. Much more crucial. And you won't get to any sort of resolution in your first conversation – so don't go in expecting this to be a one-off.

Taking the time to check in as a partnership is important on a number of levels. Money is just one of them, and most of the conversations we all have about money are usually about what bills are coming in, and who is paying what by when. They are very transactional and don't really give either partner a chance to voice their goals, dreams, or worries when it comes to money and how things are tracking for you.

So this is it. Relationship dream time. This first meeting needs to be the start of a two-way, ongoing dialogue. How's it been for you? What are your frustrations or fears around money? What would you love to do? Together or separately? The aim of this session is to talk about the bigger picture of life and money. And it will only be effective if both of you go into it committed to being honest and open.

YOU

Okay, I'm glad we are doing this.

YOUR PARTNER

Well, I am glad we have this beer and cheese platter.

YOU

Me too. So, I will start. My big dream is to buy a home. I am so sick of not having a garden and being able to put pictures on my walls.

$\longrightarrow$

YOUR PARTNER	Yes, a garden would be good. But a mortgage? I grew up in a family that was a slave to the mortgage. Not keen to repeat that.
YOU	Hmm. Okay. Well, I guess we would have to be able to afford it. I figured out we would need a $100,000 deposit to start to look.
YOUR PARTNER	What! How are we ever going to save that?
YOU	I am not sure. We would have to figure it out together. But first, do you even want a home that's ours?
YOUR PARTNER	I am actually happy living close to work and renting. We would have to move way out to buy.
YOU	That's true. Maybe we could look around here and see what things cost.
YOUR PARTNER	Looking would not hurt, I guess.
YOU	Okay, deal. We can look for six months and assess again where we are at.
YOUR PARTNER	Sounds good. Cheers to that.

> **HAPPILY EVER AFTER BEGINS WITH A BRAVE CONVERSATION AROUND MONEY. AND ALSO TIME. YOU CANNOT CHANGE MINDSETS QUICKLY. EACH CONVERSATION HAS TO BE ABOUT PROGRESS, NOT THE FINAL SOLUTION.**

MODERN MONEY RELATIONSHIPS

So much has changed societally in the way men and women interact about money.

Talking about money with our partners is actually quite a new thing, historically speaking. Our grandparents and their parents would have rarely, if ever, talked about money together. Our own parents would have found a simple system that worked for them early on, and that was that.

When I was growing up, Dad was the money earner and Mum would manage it and buy what we needed. As far as I know, they didn't discuss it further than that, except when big purchases like a holiday came up. Having regular check-ins about the finances wouldn't have been a thing. They would have known what was coming in and what bills needed to be paid, and would have occasionally made a decision to buy something. One would have said, we can afford it, or we can't, and that would have been that.

These days, the typical conversation isn't about what one partner is willing to give the other as housekeeping money, it's whether a couple will open a joint bank account. Many couples keep their finances separate nowadays, especially millennials. Some couples have had other long-term relationships, have kids with an ex-partner, maybe own their own house already, or have some other investments or properties stashed away, before they found each other.

This means that we also come to our relationships with a whole bunch of financial baggage and beliefs about money. We've written an entire collection of our own stories about money growing up, and we bring all this into our relationships.

Something that is crucial to figure out before committing to a partner is how financially compatible you are with them and what it means for your relationship. Do you have the same ideas and values about money, or are you on completely different pages? Do you even want the same things? It's so important to iron this out now.

If you can get that right, you will save yourself a whole lot of heartache later down the track, when you wake up and realise you were not a match made in heaven after all. It's always better to know up front.

Talk Soon, Talk Often
Whether you're in a new relationship or you've been together a while, it's always a good idea to have regular money talks, after you have your first "deep dive" session. It doesn't need to be boring with spreadsheets; you can pour a wine (if you drink) or order takeout together and make it fun. It doesn't matter how long you've been together. You can use it as a chance to get to know each other more. It's a good opportunity to check in and iron out some money tension that may be lingering.

YOU	Hey, here's wine. Let's chat about where we are at this month with money.
YOUR PARTNER	Really? Can't we just watch Netflix?
YOU	Well, I had some good news. I checked out our shared account and we have $150 more left over this month than I budgeted for. We can add that to our holiday account.
YOUR PARTNER	Oh. Well, that's good. Actually, I forgot to tell you, I won't drive to work anymore. Petrol's too expensive, so I will catch the train. So that's another $100 a week we can put to good use.
YOU	Wow, great idea! We are killing this budgeting thing.
YOUR PARTNER	It feels good to know we are kicking some goals. Let's cheers to that.

The earlier you can get on the same page and start talking openly and honestly about money, the better off you will be in the long run. Because this is really about aligning your personal values and goals together and supporting each other through whatever life throws at you. If you avoid these conversations, things can turn really sour, especially if they're left under the rug for quite some time.

FOR RICHER
OR FOR POORER

I've seen situations where couples didn't talk about their finances and one half just assumed the other had it under control, and it led to a literal catastrophe later on.

I once sat next to a lady on a flight who told me she had lost all her money in her fifties, including her hard-earned business, because she assumed her husband had the finances all under control. Well, he didn't – things slipped, and she wasn't aware early on, and they lost everything.

She was smart and had a successful career spanning many decades and would have been set to retire comfortably – if only they had talked about their money situation sooner and tried to figure it out together. Her husband was too proud to talk about it, and she just assumed everything was okay. While they didn't divorce, their story is a familiar one – and the reason why one in three marriages end in divorce.

Now in her mid-sixties, that lady was still working and trying to build some retirement savings for them both so they can stop working. That's an incredibly difficult position to be in, hustling in your sixties when you should be enjoying retirement.

The younger you can start thinking about what you want from life and how to get it, and be willing to talk openly with your partner about what's really going on, the stronger your wealth strategy, your partnership, and ultimately your life, is going to be.

This is why you need to start having these conversations with your partner *now*.

Financially Dependent Partners
Once upon a time, women relied heavily on their father and husband for financial security. Often, women got married purely for economic security. Not anymore.

In fact, these days women make up half of today's workforce and some out-earn their partners, and a lot of the time women are the ones who manage the finances in the home.

However, even though women have more access to finances and making money, they can still lack confidence about looking at the bigger picture.

Perhaps there are bigger problems going on. Maybe you have stuck around in an unhappy relationship, maybe because you feel financially dependent or you're sticking it out for the sake of your kids. It may be even more serious and involve abuse and financial manipulation.

If you feel stuck, I want you to know that you that you have options. You don't need to just live with it, and it's not too late to make a change. Take note that whoever controls the money controls you. So, if you don't have a say in your finances, you need to start having one.

Want that divorce? To live in a different city? Start your own business? Sell your house or buy one? Live in a different country or travel? To finally take control of your finances instead of burying your head in the sand? You absolutely can. Money controls the decisions we can make, so if you can figure your finances out – and I am going to help you do that – you can find a way to make whatever you want happen.

The Role of Money Manager

There is usually a chief financial controller in the house – someone who looks after the budget and the expenses. In my house, it's me, and that works well for both of us. As long as both partners are in agreement and talk openly about the finances and share what's going on, there's no problem. You just need to be transparent and open with each other and figure out a system that works well for both of you. If you are the one that likes admin or detail, put your hand up. If you want the job, you need to prove that you are the best placed for it. Discussing this sooner rather than later can lead to better relationships with clearly defined roles for money.

So, what does the day-to-day money situation look like for you and your partner? Who's the financial controller in your relationship? Do you have separate bank accounts or combine everything together? How do you manage the expenses? Do you know what each of you earns and what you do with your money?

Maybe your partner has been managing the finances all along, and you wouldn't mind having a bit more insight into how it's run. There's no right or wrong way to do this. Just figure out a system that works for you both. But make sure it feels fair, and don't assume roles. Ask each other what you each would like to manage in a fair way.

YOU Babe, I know you pay all our bills when you are at work. I would like to get across what our monthly costs are. Can you share the bills with me as they are paid?

YOUR PARTNER I'm handling it. You don't need to waste your time as well.

YOU Well, I am really wanting to learn more about money, and this book I am reading says this is a good place to start.

YOUR PARTNER Well, okay. I will leave the bills on the kitchen bench when I have paid them.

YOU Okay, great. I can start a file for them, and list all our costs for us to go over.

YOUR PARTNER Okay, I guess.

Perhaps you don't have shared finances yet, or maybe it's something you always want to keep separate. If it works best for you and your partner to have your finances separate rather than combined in joint accounts, that's fine too. You've just got to talk about all that openly, if you haven't already. If you haven't combined finances yet but think it could be a good idea, is now the time to have that conversation?

YOU	Hey, I notice we got the electricity bill. Rather than just giving me your half, do you want to start a joint account for bills?
YOUR PARTNER	Why? It works this way. We both pay our way.
YOU	True. It might just be easier to have something together where we can both contribute.
YOUR PARTNER	I hadn't thought about it. Maybe. Let me think about it for a while.
YOU	Okay. Sounds good.

Note that the conversation ends here. Why? Because some people take longer than others to take to new ideas about money. It is much more effective to start the conversation, and then wait days or sometimes even months, depending on the conversation's importance level, before it comes up again. Give your partner room to think about their views and form a new opinion. They may even need to talk to someone else to get clear on why they have the reaction they do. Money conversations are not fast, and should be a continued dialogue over your lifetime, not a one-conversation result.

If you've been managing your own finances individually all along, maybe you'll learn something from each other about how the other does things. You would be surprised how many couples don't even know that their partner has stocks or an investment strategy that the other doesn't know about. Even sharing a simple budgeting spreadsheet can be really powerful.

Money and Conflict

If we think about what money stories we bring into our partnerships, it's understandable why so many couples have differences and fight about money. We argue over finances for many reasons, but at the core it's because we have a different set of beliefs about money and we're not on the same page with our values and goals.

We don't agree on what we're spending money on because our values are mismatched and we're probably not working toward the same things. Add to the mix not talking about it, and you've got a disaster on your hands.

YOU	What's that you are watching on your phone?
YOUR PARTNER	NBA finals. Why?
YOU	Isn't that the pay channel that costs a couple of hundred bucks?
YOUR PARTNER	What does that matter? I love watching basketball.
YOU	Well, I thought we were saving for a house. Is that a necessary expense?
YOUR PARTNER	My happiness is necessary. So yes.
YOU	Okay. I guess I will spend on my happiness too.

There are no winners in this conversation. Why? Because a spend has been made or decided upon without consulting the other. If your partner consults you before spending, how often would you say yes anyway? The key to couples finding a harmonious balance is to talk about it before it happens. And also think about your response. Do you really need to go spending money that doesn't serve your greater goal in return?

> **YOU** — I was surprised you signed up to that cost without telling me. But I do know how much you love basketball, and you work hard, so it is a good stress release.
>
> **YOUR PARTNER** — Thanks. I have been stressed more than usual at work, so watching the game is a way of me completely switching off. But I should have told you. I will next time.
>
> **YOU** — Thanks, babe. I'll do the same. We will get that house in a couple of years at this rate. We are doing well.
>
> **YOUR PARTNER** — Yep, we are making progress.

Ending any money conversation on a positive note makes it far more likely that another conversation will be on the cards. Making each encounter a battle makes it far less interesting for your partner to take part.

When anyone gets defensive around their spending, it is because they don't want their spending decision questioned. So when you are a couple, it works to have some guidelines around the amount each one can spend without telling the other. Whether that amount is twenty dollars or a thousand, if that is known up front and respected, you are more likely to avoid conflict.

There might also be a financial imbalance because one partner earns more than the other, or one partner has a paying job and the other doesn't, or if one partner comes from a family with money and the other doesn't. These imbalances can seriously affect the relationship if you have not decided together the best way to tackle them.

> *Russ standing in their daughter's bedroom with Karen.*
>
> RUSS
> Why does Mallory have another pair of trainers? Didn't she get some last month?
>
> KAREN
> Yes, these are for netball.
>
> RUSS
> Surely the several pair of shoes she already owns can cover it?
>
> KAREN
> I made the call when she asked. You weren't here, and she was at the mall.
>
> RUSS
> Exactly. I was at work to pay for them. Which I am getting pretty sick of doing.
>
> KAREN
> I'm sorry. I will check next time. *(Guilty)*
>
> RUSS
> Thanks. *(Walks out)*

While Russ is undoubtedly a great husband and father, his views around money and spending have been deeply shaped by a childhood where he went without. His father was very tough and could be physically violent with him and his mother, particularly when he was stressed about money. Russ always vowed to never turn out like him, and he hasn't. In fact, his own kids think of him as a teddy bear. But deep down he knows that, by telling Karen he was the one at work, he was making her feel guilty for making spending decisions. She never really wastes money, and he knows her guilt will stop her from spending on other things that she should be able to decide on. Russ knows this is a form of control with money. It is subtle, but effective. He loves his wife, but he never wants to feel like he is out of control with money. He needs to feel safe. He feels safe when he is in charge.

For Karen, it is her lack of self-esteem about what value she brings to the relationship that has her reacting with guilt. She has always felt she was "just a mum," and her parents raised her to believe that would be her most important role. She is incredibly proud of all three of their children, but has always been secretly disappointed at what she has achieved herself. She has lived her life to facilitate the success of everyone else in her family. She has played a vital role for all those who benefited, but she also left herself with little super and no work experience. Her reaction to Russ saying he is sick of paying for things is a direct result of her negative self-image. She feels she isn't bringing enough to the table, and feels guilty that Russ has to do it all. What would she do without Russ? She shouldn't make decisions on spending for things without him.

In reality, what transformed Karen's life was her decision to invest in herself and start her own online business. She was a fountain of information about schools, kids, and how to do it right. An online website selling her tips and tricks, as well as recipes and how-tos, became a hit, and her income allowed her the confidence to have a say in their financial future.

Both of them had habits and beliefs that drove their behaviour. It was only through conversations with friends and an adviser that a way forward for Karen was decided upon, and by Russ supporting it, they were able to change the power dynamic in their financial relationship. Karen and Russ have a great marriage. Not always perfect, but its strength always lay in the ability for both of them to be flexible enough to work through their challenges, together but also apart.

Of course, every relationship is different. Only you know your dynamics. If you want things to change, then dealing with conflict is a great way to start. Think about what your trigger points are in your conversations. Think about how you can defuse those trigger points with a different approach or reaction. And really think about what the underlying emotion around the issue is. Is this something deeper? I am a strong believer in relationship therapy or counselling. My husband and I have been there several times over the course of our marriage, and I expect we will many more. Open conversations with a facilitator can be an incredibly powerful way to inspire behaviour change in a relationship. Seeing someone else's point of view in a new way is enlightening.

Starts with Russ at breakfast pouring Karen a coffee.

KAREN   I am meeting Josie for lunch today. We are going to talk about me possibly starting an online business, around advice for mums.

RUSS   Really? What bought this on?

KAREN   I've been thinking about it for a while. I want to make some money. Take some of the pressure off you.

RUSS   Wow. Okay. I've been happy to do it, you know. Most of the time.

KAREN   I know. You've been a great provider. But I want to feel that too. It's time for a change as the kids get older.

RUSS   I can understand that. In fact, it sounds good.

KAREN   Imagine me bringing home the bacon.

$\longrightarrow$

> **RUSS**   Babe, I have always admired your rump...
> *(moves in a for a squeeze)*
>
> **KAREN**   Russ! *(She mock-pushes him off, with a smile on her face, knowing he is getting lucky tonight.)*

Embracing new ways to encourage more money conversations in your relationship, and focusing on each interaction having a positive outcome, can be a game-changer. The secret is going in with a potential upside, not just the complaint. Karen was making a positive statement – enlisting her entrepreneurial best friend Josie to help make her online business happen. She did not go to Russ complaining about her lack of equality or say. She went in with action about changes she was making for herself. When Russ saw this, he realised that it mattered to Karen more than he knew that she contributed financially. He then realised he had been lucky to have the opportunity to have a career and create a feeling of security for himself and for his family.

They had three lovely kids who were a credit to them both. It is not easy to raise three relatively well-adjusted teens in this day and age. He knew Karen had done the hard yards for each of them by being their advocate at school, in their sports, and in their friendships. Everyone had their fair share of opportunities in the family, including him, because Karen made it happen. He just paid for it all.

It's great when a power imbalance is recognised and perceptions are shifted. It can make your relationship so much sweeter, and give it room to breathe, helping you find ways to enjoy being together, be committed to the same goals, and grow, both together and individually.

MONEY NARRATIVES IN PARTNERSHIPS

What is it that you're actually arguing about when it comes to money? What keeps coming up time and time again? Is it someone's spending habits? Is it the lack of savings you have? Is it the passive judgement you get every time an online package is delivered to the house? Or how much you're spending on the kids?

How your parents talked about money and their roles in life has made an impact on you. Equally, what your partner says, and the influences they've had from their own life, also enter the picture.

One of my characters, Jasper, would have made a pretty difficult partner when it came to money. His father had been a work addict, chasing the dollar to buy security for his family. Jasper grew up without his father's attention or time, and it deeply affected the way he went about building his own adult life. From job to job, party to party, Jasper wanted to be nothing like his father. When it came to relationships, this led to breakups and disappointment.

Everyone has a story, and until you open up the conversation about that, nothing in your relationship will change.

Money Has Emotional Roots
The beliefs and the social conditioning we talked about earlier are the thoughts we bring into our relationships too. It's important to remember that it's not just ourselves but also our partners who brings their own beliefs and taboos about money into the partnership. When these two sets of beliefs come together, if they're not aligned, they can cause friction.

Your money problems in your relationship often stem from deep emotions you've both held onto. The underlying issues we fight about are never truly about the money at all, they're about something deeper – our values, beliefs, hopes, dreams, and fears.

The emotions we attach to money and the stories we believe about ourselves, such as whether we think we're generous or successful, are tied to feelings of self-worth. The feelings of shame, envy, resentment, anger, and blame that we hold onto regarding money are stories we've created from deep-seated beliefs acquired in childhood.

FINANCIAL ALIGNMENT WITH YOUR PARTNER

The only way to address these issues is to get talking about it. If you're in a committed relationship, you and your partner owe it to each other to have a calm and honest conversation about each of your finances, habits, and upbringing – and any anxieties or worries you have around money.

Money is never just about money. It's about what money represents.

Sharing Your Money Mindsets

When you're on the same page as your partner and you're heading in the right direction, life feels so much easier. You'll probably have fewer arguments about money because you'll agree on how money is being spent.

But now is the time to get clear on your goals together. And just a heads-up: you may not agree, and your goals may clash. You're about to find out. This is why it's so important to talk.

Are you both happy in your jobs and what you earn? Do you think you should start a business together, or walk away from the family business? Do you want your partner to spend less time at work? Is work stress really getting to you? Do you each know what the other earns? What about your investments? Do you have a financial plan for the future together?

If you have kids together, do you agree on where to send your kids for school and what you want for their future? If you don't have kids, do you want to have them one day? Now is a good time to find out. Where would you want to send them to school? What does having a family look like to you? What do you envision as your parental roles and responsibilities within the family? Would you want to leave your kids an inheritance or keep the money for yourself to enjoy your life?

What are some things you truly enjoy doing together, and how can you find a way to do more of that? Even if you think some of these things don't have anything to do with money, how you spend your time is usually what you're spending your money on.

What about what you want life to look like in five or ten years? Do you want to buy a house, sell your house, or go live overseas? Do you want to be in the same job, or would you want to make a career change? Start setting some big-picture goals together, so you can get on the same page and start working together toward the future you both want.

By the way, don't assume anything your partner hasn't actually told you. You can't assume that one of you will stop working when the kids come along, or that your other half is going to take care of the retirement savings. We can't assume both partners will be equal breadwinners, or that you both want to raise your kids in the same suburb or city or send your kids to the same school. One of you might want a house in the suburbs, while the other wants an annual holiday and a holiday shack somewhere by the coast. You might really surprise each other. How exciting is that?!

One thing I would say to everyone is you need to know your money position clearly. This is one of the most important parts of putting everything out on the table. It's where you get practical and can start planning a shared future together.

I always look at money as an opportunity to get closer in a relationship and have common goals you can work toward. If you're working toward the same goals, you don't need to lie to each other and can enjoy the process as you're working toward the bigger picture.

Regardless of whether your partner has it covered, you've got to ask the questions. You don't have to take over paying the bills, but ask questions like what retirement fund are you with, what debt do you have, what have we got to pay off, and what holes do we have in our finances?

'Til Debt Do Us Part
While it might look glamorous on the outside (and on social media) to have shiny new cars, a big house with a pool, expensive clothes, and resort-style holidays, if you can't really afford it, you're going to feel miserable. There are so many people driving around in new cars they've financed on a loan, buying clothes and shoes on credit, and going on holidays that they can't really afford.

It's so easy to fall into the trap of wanting things we don't need and feeling like we need material things to make us feel happy and worthy.

*Josie ringing Karen from her hotel room
in New York.*

JOSIE   Hey, early bird. Knew you would be up.

KAREN   Yes, getting my moment of silence and
coffee before getting the kids up.

JOSIE   I just got back from lunch at Carbone with
clients. Saw Salma Hayek there!

KAREN   Wow. Sounds incredible. I'm currently
eating low-fat cereal. General consensus is
cardboard.

JOSIE   Yeah, well, clients expect to go to the best
places. Lunch cost me nine hundred dollars.
But they will spend up when they sign, I will
make sure of it.

KAREN   Well, you are very generous. You are always
buying people lunch. You should make
someone else pay every once in a while.

JOSIE   Yes, that would be nice. *(Sighs)* I have still
got a finance meeting with the team back
home tonight to get through. I know they
are going to tell me we are short of making
budget again.

KAREN   Sounds like you have a lot on. You need a
rest. Come and hang here with me and the
kids while Russ is away when you're back.

JOSIE   Sure. If I can swing a day off work, then I will.
I have back-to-back meetings for the first
few weeks back. We have a new client who
is launching a very big business.

$\longrightarrow$

KAREN	You are amazing, girl. Don't wear yourself out. Love you lots.
JOSIE	Love you too. Kiss those godchildren of mine. *(Hangs up, and goes back to her laptop.)*

From the outside, Josie's world looks amazing. She drives an Aston Martin, lives in a gorgeous terrace in Paddington that she owns, and travels the world for her work. She is fit and immaculately dressed.

But the reality is, the pace at which Josie has to work to make her business profitable means she rarely has time for anything else.

She never imagined she would not have children. It just didn't happen for her. Brad was the one who got away for Josie. No man ever came close to him after that. Josie lives in a high-pressure world, where a big win could catapult her to an even higher level of wealth, but a couple of losses could be detrimental to the point of losing it all.

It was a fine line to tread for Josie – spending money on clients that hadn't signed yet, and keeping up appearances, even when the budgets were coming in under.

She rarely slept a full eight hours; her sleep patterns were broken by travel and work demands. What had once taken her a few hours to do now took her twice as long, when it came to writing. Her head had slowed down, and she found herself often distracted by her phone, where she would just scroll mindlessly, or gazing out the windows. And of course dreaming of Brad.

The fire in her belly to succeed and grow her business had turned into a lump. She went about the motions, but it all felt in slow motion. She suspected she had depression, but fought off those thoughts, going to sleep with a gin and tonic in her hand after tossing and turning. Josie needed a way out, and it was only when she spoke to her old school friend Ben, and they talked through a way she could relieve the pressure of her cash flow and slow down, that she found it.

There's nothing worse than the stress of financial debt. If you have debt, it's time to make a plan to pay it down, and if that means selling some things, or reassessing how you're spending and change your habits so you only spend what you can truly afford, it's worth it.

GETTING SUPPORT WITH MONEY MANAGEMENT

Collaborating with a Financial Adviser

At this point in the journey, I am going to share with you one of the biggest things that changed my financial future.

My husband and I picked the right financial adviser. That's it.

The best thing we did was find the right adviser. It was through this move that we were able to come up with a solid action plan, one that gave both my husband and me total peace of mind about our future across all scenarios. I am going to help you identify the right financial planner for you in the last chapter of this book.

The process we went through with the adviser was fascinating, and it included a lot more couples counselling than you might expect, because it was really about aligning our shared goals. We needed to ask the big, hard questions to get to an actionable plan we could agreed on.

Some of the traditional financial planning questions were: Who would get the kids if we both died? (Always a fun way to start a meeting.) What money would we leave to individual family members? And how much money would we leave for the kids?

Once we hashed these out (and boy, was that an interesting process), we could then set up some more solid actions that took us toward our financial goals. It didn't happen overnight; it took a few months, because there was a lot to think about.

FINANCIAL ADVISER TAKEAWAYS

Some other questions the financial adviser asked that got us thinking were:

- How long would it take us to pay off our credit cards and never rack them up again?

- Could we get together three months' worth of emergency savings in a high-interest account and never touch it unless we were burning?

- Could we put away money every month that earned compounding interest for our kids' future, including university fees and cars?

- How much fun money did we really need to have a good life every month?

- What other investments could we add to the mix, and how much should we invest?

- What's our plan for life insurance, estate planning, and our wills?

Doing this together with a financial planner was one of the best things we did. I know it doesn't sound fun, but we learned a lot about each other, and it brought us closer together. It also solidified the future goals we were both working toward and straightened out any money issues we were having.

While I have been in the financial services industry for well over twenty years and probably knew the investing part pretty well, the other steps were the ones I needed to take to get my financial plan back on track.

These things don't all happen in a matter of weeks or even months. A cascading plan like this takes years to achieve – but with a plan, you can tick the list off, knowing that you are moving closer to the future you want. And with a solid plan, you're much more likely to get there.

I can say without reservation that a great adviser can be a brilliant asset to your life, and it doesn't matter how much you earn or how many assets you have.

Reevaluating Success and Security

While I was not able to change everything about my life all at once, the first and most important thing we did was to come to the realisation that the house and all the stuff we were buying was not what was making us happy. Being with our kids and enjoying time with friends and family was where the joy was.

We also wanted to change the way we worked and wanted the freedom to not do work we no longer enjoyed. This meant we had to undo all the things we had set up about our lives. We sold our big house, paid our credit cards down to zero, and worked toward eventually owning our cars outright.

Now, I am not saying it was fun, and there was definitely stress along the way, along with a fair amount of swallowing pride. It took five years to really turn it all around, and we had many nights wondering if it was all worth it. This part is tough, because it is not fast. The only thing that can keep you going is a clear picture of your goals, why you are doing this, and what it is going to be like on the other side. And be prepared to carry your partner over emotional hurdles sometimes too. You are both going to have to be each other's support wagon.

Another big decision we made was to move out of the city for five years, so we could raise our three sons for a large part of their schooling life in a relaxed country environment. We also built a safety-net account that will let us live for six months if no money comes in the door at all, and got our insurance and estate planning in order. All these decisions took time, effort, and a united front. If we were not on the same page, they could not have happened.

It was all definitely worth it. In the end, we got to focus on all the things that were important to us – each other, our family, friends, more rewarding work – and reduce our debt significantly at the same time.

The Truth about Retirement
Making sure you can enjoy life when you're older should be at the top of your priorities, even when you're young. Especially when you're young. Having retirement savings – and having enough – is incredibly important. The earlier you start, the better off you'll be.

The expectation of governments is that Gen Xers like me will largely self-fund their own retirements, but it is clear from the research that this financial trajectory is not looking good.

That's because the pension today covers only about a third of what is considered a "comfortable lifestyle" in retirement, and who knows where this will end up by the time the next generation is ready to retire. And by "comfortable," this doesn't mean piña coladas on the beach every day. This means being able to put food on the table and put the heater on in winter.

> **WE NEED TO GET REAL ABOUT WHAT RETIREMENT LOOKS LIKE FOR YOU AND YOUR PARTNER AND HOW YOU CAN ACHIEVE THE LIFESTYLE YOU WANT TO LIVE, BEFORE IT'S TOO LATE.**

The reality is, we're millions off from where we need to be to have a comfortable retirement. Most people are not likely to have anywhere near what they need. In twenty years, when Gen X and Gen Y will be close to retiring, a comfortable self-funded retirement is likely to require a savings balance of anywhere from one to two million dollars. These are Australian figures, but it's not much different in the US and other parts of the world. Looking at these figures, most people won't achieve a comfortable retirement at all, it's sad to say.

While the pension was put in place in 1935 in Australia and 1875 in the US to safeguard the elderly from living in poverty, it's no longer practical or sustainable in our modern lifestyles as we live longer and technology advances.

We can't assume that putting away a sliver of our wage over thirty years or so in the workforce is going to get us through a retirement that's looking like two or three decades long as we now live to eighty-five or even ninety-five years old. And that's not counting the loss of work years – and therefore retirement contributions – for women due to having children and staying at home, as well as anyone who falls ill and becomes unable to work for a period of their life.

If you don't have enough accumulating in your pension – which most of us don't – you're going to have to look outside the box. That means investing smartly and considering how you can make a side income so you can put a bit more away.

Review your accounts to see how much you have sitting in your retirement savings. If you don't know how much you have, how much you're putting away, and how much you need to retire comfortably, you need to start investigating.

> IT'S NOT TOO EARLY TO TALK ABOUT YOUR RETIREMENT AND WHAT YOU WANT LATER IN LIFE, NO MATTER YOUR AGE, HOW MUCH YOU EARN, OR HOW LONG YOU'VE BEEN IN PARTNERSHIP.

Sharing Your Values
Getting aligned with your partner starts with talking about what you agree on and disagree on and what matters to you at a soul level. It's how you can figure out if you are financially compatible with your partner.

When you're first meeting someone and you're falling in love, you're not likely thinking about their pension fund or savings plan, are you? (I don't know about you, but this is certainly not where my head was at when I met Woody.)

Once you've gotten to know each other a bit and have figured out the little quirks, like whether they lovingly leave the toilet seat up or down, how do you confront some of the deeper things about their nature? You might know how they like their coffee in the morning, but have you thought about whether they're a spender or saver? How do you start those conversations to work out whether they're going to be a good match for you in the long run, not just romantically but also financially?

Money problems, whether they crop up early in the relationship or don't surface until later, need to be confronted, because they rock the core of our essential human need: security. The number one thing we really want in a relationship, more than anything, is a solid foundation of love and security.

These are the sorts of conversations you've got to start having now. And the sooner the better. If you realise your values aren't aligned early on, that's a good thing, because now you know. And it might be time to let go if they don't match up, or, if you're willing to, work on it. If you want children and they don't, if you have goals to travel and that's not on the cards, then some of your core values, like family and adventure, might go unfulfilled. By understanding what's important to you, you can then figure out whether the same applies to your partner's core values.

MONEY AS A CATALYST FOR CHANGE AND DECISION-MAKING

Surviving Amid Global Chaos

Let's take a little pause to acknowledge that the world we live in is currently going through a tough time. Just when we thought we were coming out of a long pandemic, there have been natural disasters and international conflict, and we're still making our way through COVID-19. It hasn't been an easy time, and we can't escape the impact this is having on us.

If it's not the pandemic, lockdowns, and the disastrous effect that's all having on businesses around the world, it's environmental disasters like bushfires and hurricanes and climate catastrophes.

We're living in a time of prolonged uncertainty, and it has massively affected our lifestyles and our work and money situations. That also means the narratives we've built up about money just got a whole lot more complicated with what's been happening in the world right now.

If you were already worried about money before the pandemic, there is a big possibility that you have even more anxiety about your financial future now. A lot of couples are bearing strain and less income since COVID-19 hit, and then the outcome for that is tension and problems bubbling under the surface at home and at work.

Our mental well-being is really tied to our financial well-being, because nothing is more stressful than money problems. It's okay to talk about money and your worries. This is actually an opportunity to re-plan your life. If ever we're getting an opportunity to wipe the slate, it's now. The pandemic has changed how we work and where we work. Give yourself and your partner permission to change. Support each other through it. Be a united front.

You have the power to write the next chapter and have a say in how you live and work, what you do to have fun, and how you choose to spend and save your money. It's an important time to make plans for the unexpected. Focus on what's in your control, and plan instead of panicking.

If one of you loses your job (or already has), it's important to ask, not just what you can cut down on, but how you can best support each other during these tough times.

Not Exactly Two Peas in a Pod
Well, we said it at the beginning. Money problems cause a lot of breakups and are a big reason people get divorced. If you've figured out that you are really not on the same

page, then maybe you've come to the conclusion that it's not going to work out after all.

Which brings me to the cost of divorce. While I'm not saying it's going to happen, estimates say that around half of couples do. An older man came up to me when I was sitting in a café with my husband and said, "Never get divorced, love." My response was, "Oh, because of love?" and he said, "No, for money." Poor guy. He said he had been divorced twice and it had decimated him.

An interesting perspective is that money can sometimes motivate you to stay together and make it work because it costs too much to split up. I'm not saying that's what you should do if you're unhappy, obviously. But you should definitely just think it through before packing your bags and storming out (and if you do, take this book with you).

I've got friends who've been divorced, and they will never fully recover financially. They've made it work, but it means that, instead of living in the big house, they're living in a smaller apartment, and, instead of owning, they're renting, so they don't have an asset at the end – and they've had to split their retirement savings.

Before making a decision about something as big as this, come back to your ten-year plan. If what you want long-term isn't here, it might be time to move on.

Some people can't stay for a range of reasons. If things really aren't working, it's time to consider other options. Remember, your happiness and mental wellness come first. But it's also important to go about the process of separation in the most cost-effective way you can. Nobody wants the lawyers to get more than either of you.

You might consider speaking with a relationship therapist, a financial planner, or a money coach to help you figure things out financially. Having these mediated conversations about money may help you work through the challenges in your relationship. Whatever you do, I hope you work it out in the way that's best for you both. Some of the questions at the end of this chapter can help you both get clear what it is you really want from life.

Contemplating Marriage?

Okay, I know we just talked about divorce, but before you get married, there are a few things you've got to consider, and it's not what you're going to wear or whether you're going to serve up fish or chicken to the guests that you should be thinking about. On top of considering whether you're a good match to spend the rest of your lives together and whether you have the same ideas about what you want in life, you should probably also consider a prenup.

I know it's not the most romantic thing to be thinking of, whether you will split up after you vow to be together 'til death do you part. But it's probably a smart thing to consider to protect yourself and your finances later on in life.

I've seen too many people, both men and women – especially older women – who've told me that they've lost everything because of a divorce. This kind of thing can leave people with nothing to their name, not even a house to live in, so it is something you should absolutely consider.

Whether you're married, de facto, or haven't been together long, it's a good idea to talk about pre-nups. It's essentially an asset agreement made *before* you get married – prenup as in pre-nuptials – where you decide on which assets you own individually and which ones are shared. It's worth having a conversation and being transparent with each other.

A prenup allows you to decide what's yours if things don't work out *before* things don't work out. If you've got some assets, such as property, an inheritance, some savings or a business, it's worth looking into a prenup before you enter into a marriage contract, to protect your future self and all you've worked hard for.

If you're already married, it's not too late to get a prenup. And if you're in a long-term or de facto relationship, you can also get one. Your financial adviser or lawyer can help with this.

While we don't want to think of separating from our partner, it is a risk that statistically speaking could happen. Here's to hoping that it doesn't and that you can work your way through the tough times, but it's best to be smart and factor in every possibility down the track. Relationships can be tough at times, especially long marriages. You've just got to be prepared for what could lie ahead of you, that's all.

A lot of millennials are keeping their finances separate and not getting joint bank accounts even when they get married. But just because you're not sharing bank accounts doesn't mean that your finances are separate. If you're in a long-term partnership or marriage, and you haven't signed a prenup, they're still shared here in Australia. And it's not just assets, it's also debt that you've got to consider. Your partner's debts are yours too. Separating your finances from your partner's and not having a shared bank account might not protect you financially in the future. You'll do best to check with a lawyer, especially about what's relevant in your situation.

If your partner wants a prenup but you're not sure about it, take some time to hear them out and consider why it might be important for them. Weigh the pros and cons of what an agreement like this means for you. You might want to reach out to a family lawyer and get some advice. Don't feel pressured into anything. A prenup might not be for everyone. Just understand it, weigh it up, and then make a decision that you feel confident about.

There will be plenty of other tough decisions to come down the track in your marriage in the years to come – this is just one of them. Having these conversations won't ruin your relationship. You need to be able to talk about money with the person you're about to marry or have spent a large chunk of time with.

Courageous Conversation Pre-Planning
Before you dive deep into a full-on conversation with your partner, whether it's something big or small you want to bring up, you need to get clear on what you want to say and really think about your strategy beforehand. You may know exactly what you want to say, or maybe you're not quite ready to talk about everything – and that's completely fine. You just want to be clear on what

you want to talk about now and what you might save for another time.

Ask yourself, what are you holding back from saying and why? Sometimes avoidance is easier than being honest. Sometimes we don't want to face what's really going on because it's harder. It can feel like it's never the right time to bring up finances. You're afraid that if you do, the love and romance will suffer. Or that it's going to blow up into a disastrous argument. But the best thing you can do is just have the conversation.

Pre-Conversation Self Check-in

First, ask yourself what's holding you back from talking with your partner about money.

What would you say if you had the chance to sit down together, without distractions, and have a frank conversation about it?

What have you been wanting to discuss with your partner, but haven't had the courage yet?

What are you holding back from saying, and why?

Tips for Talking

Set some boundaries. Get clear on how you're going to approach the conversation. It's probably a good idea to set some boundaries before talking. For instance, are you going to set some rules, like no talking when I'm talking? (We use a lounge cushion as our "talking object." Whoever is holding it gets to speak and the cushion must be handed on for the other person to have their turn. It's a simple, visual way to hold space for the other person and really listen to each other.)

Have a strategy. Know what you're going to say and what you're not ready to talk about yet. Think about how this conversation is going to affect things and the best way to approach it.

Have an open mind. I don't really need to tell you that you're not going to agree with everything your partner thinks and says. You'll likely clash on some things, and that's normal. Even if it's hard, be open-minded and willing to really listen. Try to understand why they think the way they do. Remember what we said about where our beliefs come from. Have some compassion, and just try to hear them out. Their story is equally as important as your story.

Don't assume anything. We are quick to jump to conclusions and think we know everything about our partner, but don't assume you already know everything about them and what their reactions are going to be. There may be something they haven't told you that could change what you think, or something you say could introduce them to an idea for the first time.

Make a date well in advance (preferably with wine). Pick a time and place that suits both of you, where you can feel comfortable. It might be your favourite restaurant, and you can treat it like a date night. Or maybe it's at home together in a relaxed setting. Have the conversation in a neutral place, when you have the time and energy to focus on what each of you has to say. Try to limit distractions, such as the TV, and if you have kids try to put them to sleep first.

Try to make it fun! Put some music on, light a candle, put on your favourite robe, and make it an intimate event.

YOU
I'm reading this new book. It talks about having money conversations as a couple.

YOUR PARTNER
Really? Is that why you set this little picnic up?

YOU
Yes. I would like to start the process and ask you some questions. You get to ask me too.

YOUR PARTNER
Okay, how long does this go for? I want to watch Survivor.

YOU
Not long. Let's just start and see how we go. They have given me a list of questions to kick off.

YOUR PARTNER
Okay. Let's give it a go then.

Let's get the conversation started...

HAVE A COURAGEOUS CONVERSATION WITH YOUR PARTNER

There's a lot of ground to cover with your partner. Overall, you want to be looking at your individual beliefs that come into the picture, see where your values align and clash, figure out what's important for both of you, see what needs to change, and iron out any differences. A few surprises might come up too, so be prepared for that.

Below are sets of questions to foster the courageous conversation you need to have with your partner. They may trigger financial flashpoints for both of you.

First, get clear on your values:

- What are our individual and shared values in life? For example, is it family, education, freedom, well-being, success, achievement, or something else?

- What do we really want money for?

- On a scale of 1 to 10, how important is money to you, and why?

- After the bills and expenses are paid, where would you like to see our extra money go?

- If one of us inherited a lot of money tomorrow, what would we do with it?

Be honest with each other:

- Are there any secrets you're holding onto?

- Do you have a big money regret or mistake you made in the past?

- If I spent some money without telling you, say $1,000, how would you react? How about $10,000?

- How would you feel if I took on more (or less) ownership or responsibility in the shared finances?

- Do you have any money, expenses, or debts that I don't know about?

Tackle old family beliefs:

- Swap stories and talk about what you both learned about money growing up. Do these lessons currently serve you? Are there some beliefs you or your partner need to leave behind?

- When you were growing up, did your family talk about money?

- What's the financial baggage or beliefs about money we're bringing to the relationship?

- What can we unlearn about money to make it easier for us?

- What beliefs about success and wealth can you let go of?

Face your money fears and stresses:

- What's your biggest fear about money?

- What keeps you up at night about our finances?

- What is the top thing that stresses you out about money?

- What would we do if one of us lost our job?

- How can we reduce the stress around money?

Build good habits with money:

- Do you think we are good with our money? Why or why not?

- What could we do better?

- What would you want us to change when it comes to managing our finances?

- Do we need to reassess our savings plan?

Look at your spending habits:

- What are we spending our money on?

- Are we spending our money on the right things?

- Is what we're spending our money on making us happy?

- What spending habits can we change?

Assess your debts:

- What's our debt situation?

- Do you have any debt I don't know about?

- How many credit cards do we have, and what do we owe?

- What can we do to pay down our debts?

- What if we sold off some things to help clear the debt?

Put everything out on the table:

- How much do we each earn?

- What are our individual and combined assets and liabilities?

- What do we each have in retirement savings?

- Do we have health and life insurance, and if not do we need it?

- Do we need to get our wills sorted?

- Should we consider a pre-nup?

Look at the bigger picture:

- What do we both want in life as a long-term vision?

- What does life look like in five or ten years? What about beyond that?

- What's the bigger plan for us?

- Is it time to consider a financial adviser?

- What sort of things do we need help with?

- What are the shared goals we want to work toward together?

Plan for retirement:

- What do you want when you retire?

- When do you hope to retire?

- How much do you have in your retirement savings?

- Does one of us have less in retirement savings because of time out of work (such as when raising a family)?

- Do we need to think about pension contributions?

Evaluate the meaning of success and security:

- What are you looking for when it comes to security?

- What type of house do you want? What else do you want in life?

- What sort of financial stability do you want?

- Do we align on this? Where do we differ? Where can we find common ground?

Continuing the Conversation

Hopefully you've covered some good ground with your partner, and you've discussed some important topics. One of the important lessons I hope you've uncovered is that there is no need to hide any of your financial problems from your partner and it's okay to be vulnerable with the one you love.

The more you talk about money and how it fits into your relationship as a couple, the easier it gets. Make a habit of checking in with each other from time to time, especially as things change in life. Jobs come and go, tough times hopefully come and go, kids might come, and maybe leave one day. All of these things can change things up over your relationship, and you've got to keep the conversation going when they do.

But, whatever happens, remember to stay clear on what you both want in your life together.

THE CRUCIAL + GAME-CHANGING CONVERSATIONS YOU NEED TO HAVE WITH YOUR KIDS

3

KIDS AND
MONEY MINDSET

More often than not, kids have picked up habits and ideas about money from their parents. But it's not all about your influence. Some kids are risk-takers when their parents aren't at all, and some kids are good at saving while others love to spend, even if they've come from the same house.

Kids have their own ideas they've formed from other external influences, like their friends and social media. Their Instagram and TikTok feeds are going to tell you a lot about what influences them. In a world where we're keeping up with everyone on social media, it's worth noting that mental health is closely linked to financial health, so having sound financial well-being and spending money on the right things can really impact our kids' well-being overall.

Our innate personalities and external influences start to guide our decisions. It's important to know your kids' spending and savings habits and whether they're risk-takers or conservative when it comes to money, so you can stop unhealthy behaviours in their tracks.

> WHERE ARE YOUR KIDS GETTING THEIR KNOWLEDGE ABOUT MONEY AND WEALTH? WHAT CAN YOU TEACH THEM BASED ON WHAT YOU CAN SEE IS INFLUENCING THEM?

Your Child's Money Personality

We're all different with money, and everyone has a different money personality. How we manage money and how we like to learn about it are different, and it can make all the difference when it comes to helping to engage them in the money conversation. The better you know what their individual personality is like, the easier it will be to engage with them. Have a think about how they engage with money and whether they've picked up any habits or ideas.

There are many money personalities. And it is only by knowing your kids so well that you can recognise theirs.

A few common types are:

- The hustler, who is always looking for ways to make money and improve their money situation.

- The saver, who takes pride in being thrifty and saving their cash.

- The spender, who loves to spend all the money they get.

How can you find out if your kid is a spender, investor, or hustler? Start paying attention to their behaviours. If they get money for their birthday or from doing chores, do they want to put it in the bank straight away or go on a shopping spree and spend it? Or do they think about putting the money into something that could reap rewards, like collecting basketball cards or starting an eBay shop?

If your child is a hustler, you can get them involved in investing from an early age. You might talk to them about different companies they like that they could invest in, and show them how they can start using their savings to invest in some of these companies. It's important to explain the risks to them as well. You can find these apps online now; make sure you do your research and read reviews of each of these online trading platforms to see what works for you. Yes, that means you have to go and do your own research. Start by googling "popular online trading platforms."

I'm not going to tell you which ones to use. You need to start taking a look yourself and getting familiar with it before you start this conversation.

YOUR KID	**Nana gave me fifty dollars for my birthday, I'm getting that new game!**
YOU	Wow, that's lucky. What other money did you get?
YOUR KID	**Two twenty-dollar gift cards from my friends.**
YOU	Amazing. Happy birthday. Why not choose a game with the gift cards, and buy shares in Sony PlayStation with the fifty dollars from Nan?
YOUR KID	**I can do that?**
YOU	Yep, It's an app. I can show you.
YOUR KID	**Can I put that app on my phone so I can check it?**
YOU	Yes, with some rules around it.
YOUR KID	**Cool.**
YOU	Parenting ✓

If they're a saver, this is great! But make sure they're not scared to spend on the things they value. They might be the kind of kid who really wants something but feels guilty for spending the money. They may have picked up a lack mindset from somewhere. Get them to think about what they want, so they can put money aside for something that's important to them.

YOU	Wow, you have done a lot of shifts at work. What are you going to spend your money on?
YOUR KID	Nothing special. I'm just saving it.
YOU	Great. What are you saving for?
YOUR KID	I don't know.
YOU	Well, it's smart to save for a rainy day. Have you got a second account?
YOUR KID	Why would I?
YOU	Well, then you could move some into long-term savings, and use the everyday account for when you want something for yourself, like a birthday present for a friend.
YOUR KID	Oh, that makes sense. Thanks.
YOU	Parenting ✓

If your child is a spender, it is important to teach them to save money, as this is the personality that is the hardest to shift once it becomes ingrained. It's also important to help them realise that there is not an unlimited supply of money if they do choose to spend. Getting your kids conscious of tradeoffs and decisions now and later is a lifelong journey.

YOUR KID	I'm going to spend this ten dollars at the shops today.
YOU	What on? Is that all your pocket money?
YOUR KID	Yep
YOU	Then you won't have anything left.
YOUR KID	So, it's my money.
YOU	If we go to the mall tomorrow, you won't be able to get that cool poster you wanted.
YOUR KID	Can't you buy it?
YOU	No, it's something you wanted.
YOUR KID	Oh well, no poster I guess.
YOU	Okay. Your choice.
YOUR KID	Yes, it is. (*now understanding limited resources*)
YOU	Parenting ✓

Teaching kids about money and how to manage it is how you will set them up for a good life ahead.

LEADING BY EXAMPLE

The Parental Commitment

As parents to three boys, Woody and I can agree that having children has been the most rewarding, exhausting, forever job you could do. And the big word there is *forever*.

Like our commitment to our kids, a commitment to getting our children financially independent is one of the biggest jobs we have. Because when they are capable of creating their own income and understand how to grow their own wealth, you have done your job – to give your offspring the best chance possible, not just at survival, but at being independent and flourishing in life.

Our kids are heading closer to the young adult years, and I can safely say I now know there will never be a time when I won't be their mum, that Woody and I won't be talking about them and worrying about them as they navigate life, no matter what age they are.

> I HAVE ALWAYS BELIEVED THAT TEACHING YOUR KIDS ABOUT MONEY BY TALKING OPENLY TO THEM IS A LEGACY AND GIFT IN ITSELF.

Talking about investing and growing wealth was not part of my childhood – my parents simply didn't think like that, or really have access to that information. But they did teach the principles of saving up, and buying a home. I'm sure many of you will have had the same upbringing. We now must unlearn what we were brought up to believe, so we can have very different conversations with our kids.

> **WHETHER YOU LEAVE A FINANCIAL LEGACY TO YOUR KIDS OR NOT, THE MOST IMPORTANT THING YOU CAN GIVE THEM IS EDUCATION SO THEY CAN BECOME FINANCIALLY INDEPENDENT FOR LIFE.**

I have always asked questions when working with finance leaders about how they were raised, when they started investing, and what they taught their kids about money. What I've learned over the years from talking with hundreds of master investors is that the best way to get your kids on the road to financial freedom is to have real conversations with them about money and engage them with money as a concept from the youngest age possible.

The younger they are, the more opportunity you have to get the ball rolling with good money habits and important concepts like saving and investing.

The earlier we start the conversation with our kids, the more we set them up to have a successful financial future. And as they get older, we should keep engaging with the technology and the tools to keep them on the right track. Whether you have young kids in school, teenagers, or adult kids, it's really never too early or too late to talk to them about money.

Have you ever really had a conversation with your kids about money? What sort of things have you told them about money, even if it's offhand? What haven't you told them yet? What do your kids really know and not know about money? It's time to start having those conversations with your kids now, before it's too late. You don't have to do it all at once, but take the opportunities life presents to offer suggestions and a framework for their thinking.

YOUR KID	I've got a job at Domino's. I am going to be earning cash!
YOU	That's great. Well done for making it happen. Did you pick your super fund?
YOUR KID	What? Nah, gotta fill out the paperwork they gave me.
YOU	You want help?
YOUR KID	No
YOU	Can I send you a list of super funds to read about? They will manage your investing cash through the super you get paid.
YOUR KID	My investing cash?
YOU	Yes, that's what super is. Money invested for future you.
YOUR KID	Cool. What funds are there?

$\longrightarrow$

YOU	Here's two that I think look good for people in retail work.
YOUR KID	**They are on the list.**
YOU	Cool. Pick what sounds more like you – check out their social.
YOUR KID	**I will. Thanks.**
YOU	You won't get paid until you get that paperwork in, so do it now.
YOUR KID	**I'm busy, but fine.**
YOU	Parenting ✓

Parents as Financial Leaders

To give your kids a true understanding about money, you've got to give them an idea of where your ideas about money have come from and how you've had to earn your way. Whether you're financially successful or don't have much in your bank account, there are lessons there to teach them either way.

If you're in debt and struggling financially, maybe you could be open about it with your kids, so you can help teach them about not repeating the behaviours that got you into that situation. If you've made millions and have a bunch of assets, maybe there's a thing or two you could teach your kids about growing wealth. And if you're an average family with a mortgage and bills you're trying to keep up with every month, there are surely some lessons there that you can share with your kids about budgeting, saving, and investing.

> **YOU** — For once, I'm going to do the right thing. I will make dinner Friday night rather than buy pizza.
>
> **YOUR KID** — That sucks. We love pizza.
>
> **YOU** — Me too. But it's forty-six bucks we could use to pay down the credit card. Less interest to pay the bank.
>
> **YOUR KID** — We pay the bank interest?
>
> **YOU** — Yes. When it's credit, it's not our money. It's a loan from the bank. If you pay it in thirty days, you don't pay interest. But after that, you pay a lot more.
>
> **YOUR KID** — We should pay it back then.
>
> **YOU** — Exactly. I'll make toasties.
>
> **YOUR KID** — And I will eat them.

As parents, we want better for our kids than what we had for ourselves. We don't want our kids to learn the hard way or to suffer through financial burden. But it's important to remind our kids where we came from and the sacrifices we had had to make to get to where we are and give them the life they have. This is invaluable in giving them a bit of appreciation for what it takes to earn money and manage it. A little bit of perspective goes a long way.

Your kids might not know what it was like for you when you got your first mortgage or bought the family home, or they may not realise you were never able to buy a property. Maybe you didn't get the chance to have an education like they did, or you ate beans for three years while you were getting yourself through university or college without any help from your own parents before you got that steady job. Sharing some insights into the lessons you've learned in your own life can be some of the greatest, most valuable lessons your kids will learn.

YOUR KID I need a new pair of shoes. These are falling apart.

YOU But those are only six months old. How did this happen?

YOUR KID I dunno.

YOU I do. You jam your feet into them and break the backs.

YOUR KID Not every time.

YOU When I was a kid, I got one pair of sports shoes per year until my feet grew.

YOUR KID I'm not you.

YOU No, you seem to need more. So how about you work to fund your second pair of shoes.

YOUR KID What? No way.

YOU Yes. The car can be washed for the next two Sundays, and you can clean up the dog poo all week, plus empty the bins for recycling.

YOUR KID My life sucks.

YOU Parent Box ✓

So many people don't talk about money around the dinner table, and that means their kids aren't financially literate. The older generations may have believed it was rude to talk about money, but the reality is, if we don't open up about money with our kids, they will never be prepared for what life is about to throw at them, and managing money is going to be such a big part of that.

However old or young your kids are – or maybe you don't have kids yet, but you want to get a head start on thinking about starting a family – it's never too soon or too late to start the conversation.

It's not just about teaching your kids to save money and put it in the bank, or perhaps invest. It is about teaching them how to take care of themselves for their future and showing them valuable skills in assessing financial risk based on the life decisions they are making. It's also about helping them identify what they would really like for their future and finding a way to make that happen.

Just as your kids are with you for your lifetime, so is your opportunity to teach them valuable lessons and help guide them on their life journey. And it's no different with money education. It's a lifetime commitment, and it all starts with having the conversations with them.

As parents, I'm sure we all worry that our children may make the wrong decisions and suffer their consequences. My father, with his Serbian accent, used to tell me when we had kids to "make their life pretty." What he meant by that was to make that short time they have in childhood as wonderful as possible. Sometimes we can't stop our kids being part of terrible circumstances, but as much as you can, buffer them from the harsher realities of life while they are young. Both my parents were masters at this. While we may have had money worries growing up, neither of my parents really let on, and we lived our childhood relatively carefree, largely unaware of any stresses they had.

As we get older and so do our kids, there is still always the feeling of wanting to protect them and wanting to make sure their life is secure. Every parent wants the best for the kids. Talking about it over a period of time – over months, and years – can really create a new connection as parents and children, if we are courageous enough to put our money taboos aside and speak honestly. I want you to give your kids everything they need to set themselves up for a future that's financially independent.

I WANT TO HELP YOU TEACH YOUR KID TO BE MONEY-SMART FOR LIFE.

There are some key things I want you to think about straight up.

Leaving a Legacy Behind
If you are planning on leaving your kids an inheritance or if there is something you want to be remembered for, you've got to start thinking now about what that looks like for them, no matter how old you or they are now. Even if your kids are still fairly young, you can involve them in a conversation about their future and the legacy you want to leave them. The sooner you have the conversation, the better off you will be on both sides. Not only will they know what to expect, but you'll also know what they plan to do with the money you have worked so hard for. And if you are ahead of

the game, you can call the shots and set the agenda for a money conversation about that legacy.

Establishing Good Money Habits

Whether your kids are older or younger, you want to try to instill good habits in them. It's easier to start this early, but if you have older, adult kids, you might want to talk to them about changing some money habits you can see they've fallen into, whether it's accumulating debt or a lack of savings. These are all things you've got to be comfortable talking with them about, no matter what age they are or whether there might be different opinions flying around.

Getting Started Early

I can't stress this one enough. The earlier you start with getting your kids on track with learning about money, saving, and investing, and getting comfortable talking about it, the better off they'll be in the long run.

YOU	No, we won't be buying those candies today at the checkout.
YOUR KID	I want them! Please please please please.
YOU	No, we decided we all want ice cream, so we spent the money on that.
YOUR KID	But I want this too.
YOU	We have got to choose, and we all voted ice cream. We can take a vote next time.
YOUR KID	Grumble...
YOU	Parenting ✓

HARD TRUTHS ABOUT PARENTING AND MONEY

The Cost of Having Kids

Let's acknowledge this elephant in the room. Small humans are expensive. Keeping them alive, fed and happy can be a big part of our financial woes. We want to give everything to our kids, but that comes at a price.

A lot of parents walk around with a heavy burden of mortgage, school fees, bills, a stressful job, and a family to feed. As a parent of three boys, I know that raising kids and keeping them alive, safe, clothed, schooled, fed, and healthy isn't cheap or easy, and it doesn't exactly get any cheaper or easier as they grow into teenagers and adults. But I've come to learn that some of the best things in life aren't easy or cheap.

When you factor in the cost of school, family outings, holidays, food, and electricity bills, you begin to wonder how many grocery bills, annual school fees, and family trips could have equated to a mansion by now. I wouldn't trade it for anything in this world, because family is everything to me and our kids are our life, but I'm just saying, these kids aren't cheap.

The cost of raising just one child is about a quarter of a million dollars if you're in the Western world, like in the US or Australia, and that's just the average. That hasn't factored in whether they continue to live with you when they turn eighteen or if you're going to pay for their university or college fees. Let's face it, how many of our kids are actually going to leave home when they finish high school, unless they're going away for tertiary education?

With the rising cost of rent in cities and exploding property prices that haven't matched wages, it's becoming harder for the younger generations to move out and become financially independent until much later. Rent has exploded in big cities, with many twenty-something professionals surviving month to month in shared houses to pay rent and bills and have a social life. Some are just opting to stay at home well into their twenties and even thirties. Gone are the days when living with your parents in your mid- to late twenties was uncool; it's very common now.

It became even more interesting as the pandemic hit and adult kids, many in their thirties, had to move back in with their parents when they lost their jobs and couldn't afford to pay rent. The reality is that life is more expensive and unpredictable now than it ever was. Our kids are facing a very different world, and we need to prepare them as much as we can. The best way to do that is to equip them with the financial knowledge they simply need to know — not only to get ahead, but to survive.

Some kids won't realise how expensive life can be in the real world until they get out there themselves, especially those who've had it pretty good at home. But what you teach them early on about money will help prepare them for what's to come.

One of the best lessons you can teach your kids is that things don't come easy in life. If you expect your kids to be supporting themselves after they turn eighteen, you need to let them know about it before that time comes. But beyond letting them know, you need to help prepare them for what that looks like. This includes the simple act of having them get a part-time job as a teenager. This experience will be invaluable in teaching them how hard it is to make money and to value what you earn.

Deciding whether or not to make certain financial sacrifices as a parent to better your child's future can be a tough decision. We should be able to enjoy the money earned from our hard work, but we also want to ensure our children are provided for in both the short and long term. If your kids know you're working hard to help with their future, they might think about school a bit differently or start thinking about their own future sooner.

Some parents think they should give their kids everything, including an expensive education and lots of experiences, even if it means putting their finances on the line. Regardless of your personal stance, your family's financial situation is an important topic to discuss. There's no shame in discussing what you can and can't afford.

Every family scenario is different. However, no matter the circumstance, it's crucial that parents can have an open dialogue about money with their kids.

> **YOUR KID** Everyone is going to the mall this weekend. Can I go?
>
> **YOU** What will you get up to?
>
> **YOUR KID** Maybe go to the movies?
>
> **YOU** Do you have enough money to go?
>
> **YOUR KID** Ah, no, I spent my twenty-dollar allowance.
>
> **YOU** With your school fees and all the other bills, it's just not possible this month to give you more....
>
> **YOUR KID** Oh. Okay. I will tell them I can't go.
>
> **YOU** Or invite them over here if you like.
>
> **YOUR KID** Okay
>
> **YOU** Parenting ✓

Irrespective of age or financial situation, the most important step for parents and children alike is to start preparing for the future today.

Don't wait. Otherwise, time that could be used on the power of compounding is slipping away, and every day you wait might mean you have to make greater sacrifices tomorrow.

Don't be intimidated by it. Start learning what you can and talk about it with your kids. You'll be amazed at what can happen in just a few conversations.

The Financial Jargon Learning Curve for Parents
Of course, it's not only kids who don't understand money; it's adults too. I've spent a lot of my career trying to decipher and decode what finance people were talking about, especially when I started out as a finance journalist. I worked in institutional finance, where investing billions is part of the work, and I realised these people were speaking a completely different language from everyone else.

It feels like there are a lot of people locked out because they don't speak the same lingo as the finance experts. Finance can feel like a bit of an exclusive club. If that world is something you aren't exposed to and you haven't had the knowledge passed down to you from your parents, it can be really hard to figure out how to do it for your kids.

If you feel you're not equipped yourself and don't understand some of these basics, like how to manage your cash flow (when money comes in and out) and keep a budget, then you need to educate yourself first and then pass on your knowledge to your kids. There are plenty of tools out there, for adults and for kids, to teach you the basics of money – and I have plenty of resources on my website to help you out too.

A lot of people have been programmed with a feeling of lack, which is why they are financially conservative and think they don't have access to the things they want. Some parents project this onto their kids. You want them to save and be smart with their money, but if you're watching everything they're spending, you're not letting them develop their own money personality and their own habits.

It's okay to not know everything when it comes to finance. Most people don't. I didn't have a clue when I started out. I just talked to lots of clever people in finance and asked them to explain everything to me in layman's terms until I finally understood what they were talking about. Now we have Google and YouTube, luckily.

There are a million ways to teach yourself and your kids about the practicalities of how to make, invest, and save money. But what's more important is that you're just open to talking about it. If there's something you don't understand or that you don't know how to explain to your kids, you'll be able to find some help. When you open up the dialogue about money with kids, you'll find that it's not taboo to talk about it, and that they're not afraid of it either.

Financial Bias Ownership and Awareness
When it comes to educating kids about money, it not only starts with involving them in money discussions from a young age, it is also about being aware of how you are talking about money and being mindful of your own behaviours. That's because what you say about money and your actions around it will be picked up by your kids.

They soak it all up, from watching how you earn money to watching how you spend it. They'll take note if you're frugal or a spender, and they'll even notice where you shop and what groceries you buy for the house. They'll be aware if you spend money on yourself or not and where you take them out as a family. It won't take them long to figure out if you're an investor and if you speak confidently about money or not. They'll take in what you say about money, like if you say you can't afford something or if you point out the neighbours' fancy new car. They'll pick up your fears around money and begin to model your behaviours and your beliefs more than you'll realise. It all gets absorbed.

Starts around the breakfast table at Karen and Russ's house.

KAREN — Who left that milk splash on the table?

NATE — I dunno. Probably me. Sorry, Mum. I was snapchatting my mate Rick on his holiday, he is in Bali.

RUSS — That sounds great. Maybe we should go there.

NATE — Yeah! I would love that! Can we?

KAREN — As if we could afford Bali. We are still paying off last year's holiday. No way.

RUSS — Ever the wet blanket. Thanks, love.

KAREN — I'm just being realistic. It wouldn't hurt if I was not the only one.

RUSS — Sure. Obviously, we aren't going to Bali.

NATE
MUTTERING — Of course we aren't.

KAREN — I hate being the one that says no. Thanks, Russ. *(Walks off)*

If we're running around working long hours and coming home in the evenings exhausted, while we stress about paying bills and talk about all the financial problems we're facing and how expensive everything is, our kids take note. If your children see you investing, they'll be more inclined to replicate that; if they see you struggling, they'll probably learn a scarcity mindset and stay there for quite some time.

Take a moment to think about how the beliefs and actions of your own parents impacted you and your decisions, and you'll see what I mean. You either took on their beliefs and modelled them or decided to completely go the other way and rebel against them. Whatever you learn from your parents is usually how you end up managing money, or you rebel and do the exact opposite because you didn't like how they managed money themselves.

The more aware you can be of what you are saying about money, and about your own beliefs that are coming out in your actions, the more you can set your kids up with a financial future that's really going to benefit them.

But if you're talking about money in a way that's negative, if you're stressed about paying bills, if you're averse to taking risks, and if you don't believe you can have financial wealth, your kids are going to take that into their lives too. They'll keep living their life the way you have and will make the same mistakes until they get a wake-up call and change it for themselves.

> **YOUR KIDS' MONEY EDUCATION REALLY STARTS WITH YOU. THEY'RE TAKING NOTES ALREADY, JUST SUBCONSCIOUSLY. YOUR BELIEFS BECOME THEIRS.**

Financial Literacy Gap

Teaching your kids about money is critical for their success in life. We know that the earlier you can start teaching kids about money, the better off they'll be in the long run. It's peace of mind for both them and you to know they can look after themselves financially and that they'll be okay on their own in the real world.

Many parents feel they lack the time, knowledge, and experience to teach their kids what they need to know to be financially independent and successful. So if parents aren't teaching kids, who is?

Unfortunately, kids don't learn basic money skills at school, so many of them are clueless when it comes to money unless they've been taught at home.

We live in a financial world where all our choices come down to what we can afford, so it makes sense to instill in our kids an understanding of finance and investing, just as it does with math and sciences.

At school, our kids learn maths and more advanced algebra and trigonometry, but they don't get a financial education about budgeting, taxes, how interest rates and compound interest work, and all the different ways to invest money. While some schools are starting to teach kids about investing on the stock market, we can't really rely on the school system to teach our kids about all there is to know about money.

Ask your kids what they have learned about money at school. Get some insight into what they already know and what they don't yet. Then you can try to fill in the gaps.

THE GREAT LESSON IS
TO START EARLY

Money is sort of invisible to the younger generation because we are now mostly a cashless society. When we were kids, we used to get a few gold coins or a five-dollar note to go down to the shops or we'd buy those one- or two-cent lollies (candies for the Americans) at the local shop and count them out one by one – a hundred for one dollar. Some kids these days haven't had much exposure to notes and coins, so they literally think money is a plastic card or an app on a smartphone.

The other thing is that, for a lot of kids, it seems money is about asking a parent for some, and they'll either get a yes or no. They don't really think about getting it for themselves until they're much older. But it's a good idea to get them thinking about making, saving, investing, and managing their own money from a young age.

When they hit the teen years, you can think about getting them a bank account, even before they get a casual job. It teaches them accountability and helps them to learn to save and spend within their means. They can put birthday money in there, or pocket money from doing chores.

I believe all children should have their own account by the time they're teenagers. My boys got their bank accounts when they turned thirteen, and I really don't think that's too early. It's a good time to start when they're teenagers, because it gives them accountability and a level of control over their money while starting to teach them some important skills about the value of money they'll need for life.

My son saved up $11,000 from delivering pizzas, which blows my mind. He's saving toward a bigger goal of travel, and I think that's so cool because he's taking ownership of what he wants, and he's figured out a way to go and get it. That's what you want for your kids.

Probably the most important thing to do is involve your kids in financial conversations early on and lead by example.

PRICELESS DEPOSITS WITHIN PARENTING

Parenting ROI (Return on Investment)

As a parent, I know how much you want to give your kids everything. The truth is, the seeds you plant now with your kids can reap big rewards for them later. Giving them things as material possessions isn't going to teach them anything about the value of money. As they say, if you give someone a fish, you feed them for a day, but teach a person to fish and you feed them for a lifetime. It's the same concept here. Give them the tools they need to learn skills that will help them sail through life, and the earlier you start, the better.

You're better off teaching your kids the value of delayed gratification by saving and investing than giving them everything now, even if you can afford it. Teaching them about putting some money aside into a high-interest investment is going to be a lot more valuable later than spending it on something now.

What you give your kids over their childhood and teen years – their possessions, education, the home they live in, the family holidays you go on – and what you teach them about it will make a real difference to how they think about money and how they behave with money as they get older. It's not about giving them more; it's about teaching them about the value of money and what it can do from a young age.

Teaching Kids about Investing

When they get into high school seems to be the time most professional investors start exposing their children to investment lessons. One asset manager I worked with believed that getting kids interested in a company early on was incredibly important to spark their passion in investing from a young age. If young people have a passion or interest in an organisation, they should be encouraged to own some shares in it. So if they are into tech, they may want to invest in Apple, or Nike if they're into sports. Their passion for a product can easily become a way of starting to invest.

These lessons will stick for life, and any mistake they make along the way won't have the same repercussions it could have later in life if they were investing a lot more money. It's important to let them know that there is risk involved in investing, so they need to be okay with losing the money as a worst-case scenario.

Even though a lot of the fund managers I spoke to bought their kids shares in their early teens and got them learning about stock market investing from a young age, it was something I was initially a bit hesitant about when it came to my own kids.

But I bit the bullet and decided to do it with my eldest son when he turned seventeen. My husband and I gifted him some shares in a couple of listed companies he liked – Apple and Atlassian – as a birthday present, and it was a great decision because it got him really interested in investing and has taught him some valuable investment skills.

Understanding Compound Interest

Here's a simple explanation of compound interest for your kids (and even for yourself): Compound interest simply means that you earn "interest," which is a percentage of the savings amount. Every time you earn interest, it gets lumped into the savings amount. So that means every time interest is calculated, it's based on the new savings amount. So the earlier you start saving, the more money you're going to accumulate over time because of compound interest. It's how a thousand dollars can turn into two thousand dollars just by sitting in an investment. The earlier you put it in there, the quicker the compound interest accumulates. It can have an enormous impact in the future.

Here's a task for you. Sometime this week (or even today!), bring up "compound interest" with your kids and see what they know about it. A simple YouTube or Google search will help you find some videos if you need some help explaining it!

Explaining the Stock Market to Kids

You can start to explain to your kids that the stock market is a way of buying a percentage of a business and a share in the profits. So if a company does well and their profits increase, the share price likely goes up, and you can reap the rewards by cashing in (selling the stock) or let it continue to grow as an asset. The company might also pay dividends, which you could explain to your kids is like getting an annual bonus. The more shares you have and the better the company does, the more rewards you reap.

You can show them simple examples. Like instead of just buying the latest iPhone, you can own a share in the company and get rewarded for investing your money in the company Apple itself. Or as you walk around the aisle at the supermarket, you can explain to them that if you are a shareholder in the supermarket, you get a tiny bit of profit from the groceries you buy, which actually goes back in your own pocket as a company shareholder. These kinds of concepts blow kids' minds.

With a couple of these key investing concepts under their belt, your kids may be ready to start learning how to invest in the stock market. You can start teaching them a few investing strategies, like how to understand more about the companies before investing. My younger son likes Tesla cars, so I let him invest in Tesla using his own money. He's watched it go up and down, but it's been a lesson for him to figure out how the stock market works in real life.

It is important to teach them about investing responsibly, and, if they're young, it's got to be something you monitor. One of the most important things is to teach kids about diversification – anything else is like putting everything on black.

The logic is straightforward—don't put all your eggs in one basket.

In saying that, you've got to allow your kids to make mistakes. A baby doesn't learn to walk by being carried everywhere. You've got to let your kids make some mistakes on their own. Losing money as a kid is equally important because it makes them understand risk and makes them more likely to be a sensible investor rather than a gambler.

YOU — What's you got you upset?

YOUR KID — I bought some shares in a company with my pay, and now it's lost 30 percent.

YOU — How did you choose that company?

YOUR KID — I picked the one with the lowest share price so I could buy more.

YOU — Did you read any research or what analysts said about it? It's all on the app.

YOUR KID — No, I did my own picking.

YOU — Okay, good lesson. The stock may come back up – do your research and find out what's happening with them before you sell and lock in the loss.

YOUR KID — Yeah, okay. I should have done that first.

While it's important to explain risk, this shouldn't be about holding them back from taking a risk. Having a zero-risk mindset will see them avoid investing altogether. This means you might need to leave your own biases at the door. If you're scared of the stock market, this is going to rub off on them. Again, it's good to get your own knowledge polished up so you can feel confident about helping your kids out.

Are you ready to introduce your kids to the world of stock trading? Is it something they would be interested in? Have you taught them the basic skills of saving, budgeting, and cash flow first?

Start with the Simple Stuff
Stock market trading is only one aspect of building wealth, and it's not the same as teaching kids about saving and managing money and looking at other investments. While I think it is good to teach kids how to invest – and it's something I've got my kids doing – playing around with share trading isn't exactly teaching kids about the wider spectrum of money.

We've got to get kids thinking about their values, budgeting, savings strategies, the banking system, how borrowing money works, and cash flow.

It is never too early to start teaching kids some basics about money, and it can be really simple to start with. For example, taking the time to explain that money doesn't come out of the wall from an ATM is a good place to start. Let them know that those plastic cards you carry around have money on them that you worked hard for. It's probably a good idea to explain the difference between a credit card and debit card too.

YOU	It's time to get you your own bank account.
YOUR KID	Cool. Can I get a card so I can buy things online?
YOU	Yes, it's called a debit card. You can buy things, but only with the amount in your account.
YOUR KID	Is that what you use?
YOU	Yes. I also have a credit card for emergencies, which is the bank's money, but debit is better. You only spend what you have and don't get into debt.
YOUR KID	Okay, cool. Now I need money to put in that bank account.
YOU	Okay, time to decide chores for you. Let's make a list and negotiate a price.
YOUR KID	Okay, cool. Can payday be today?
YOU	Can you do these jobs today? If so, yes.

I think it's also important to be open about what you can and can't afford as parents and as a family. Teaching them about making a choice between a more expensive item at the store and a cheaper one is also a simple lesson they'll take with them. There is nothing wrong with explaining that they can have one thing but not the other, because the budget doesn't allow for both.

Teaching Kids about Value

One of the most important lessons you can teach your kids is to help them understand the importance of living their life according to their values. Values change at different stages of life – when you're young it might be friends and your education, and when you're older that might shift to family and health – but it's a good idea to get them thinking about their values early on. If you get them thinking about what they care about from a young age, it will help to set their priorities and curb mindless spending while getting them working toward real goals.

You want to try to get your kids thinking about things like: Why do they want money? What would they do with it if they had it? What do they actually care about more than anything?

It obviously depends on their age, but it's never too early to start instilling positive values and get them thinking more mindfully when it comes to money. Even older adult kids might need a reminder about their values.

For some kids, it could be about spending as much time with friends as possible or doing well at school. For others, they might already be thinking about having a nice house one day or going travelling or studying abroad. Other kids might want fast cars and Instagram fame. Whatever they want, you've got to ask them why.

YOU	Are you buying another game online?
YOUR KID	Yes. It's my money, so I can buy what I want.
YOU	That's true. I thought you were saving up for a car. Remember, we will match whatever you save.
YOUR KID	Hmm. True. So this twenty dollars could turn into forty if it goes in savings for the car.
YOU	Correct. You catch on fast, kiddo.
YOUR KID	Well, I am all about doubling my money. I won't buy the game. Thanks for the reminder.
YOU	Parenting ✓

This doesn't need to be serious. You can make it light-hearted and fun. It could be a few conversations in passing. The aim is to get them thinking about what they really care about by asking them some questions about what they really want and what's important to them—and don't forget to find out why.

FINANCIAL LITERACY
FOR THE FUTURE

Teaching New Kids New Tricks

One thing I want to make sure you know is that you don't need to pass on your old habits to your kids. If you've identified that you've got a bit of work to do with your own money habits or beliefs, you can start working on that to help your kids learn better ways. The best way is to lead by example, so if you've got old habits and subconscious beliefs to let go of, you can start to unlearn them and learn new ways.

Have a look back over your own past and think about what your parents (and your partner's parents too) taught you about money and what they used to say. Was there anything you picked up that isn't working for you and your family now?

The reality is that the world is a very different place now, and it will continue to be as our kids get older. Our kids are looking at a very different future. They're not going to have a job for life; we all know that because of how much work has changed now. They may never buy a house or get a mortgage because of the way the property market is going. They may put their money into a range of investments, some of which don't even exist yet.

> I WANT PARENTS TO THINK BIG WITH THEIR KIDS.

If you've been thinking small and confining your ideas to what you know and learned growing up, you're going to be limiting your kids' potential. Their potential to make money and live a fruitful life is huge. It's available to all of us. The reality is, we're facing a new world these days. We've shifted toward a cashless, digital society which has become an inevitable way of living now, and the pandemic accelerated that shift.

What the next generation will do will blow our minds. These kids are going to do lots of different things in life. For them, it's about working smart, not working harder. Teaching them different ways to make money and manage it and letting them think outside the box will be valuable for their future.

Whatever path they choose and whichever direction you guide them in, you need to start the conversation about money with them as soon as possible. Get them thinking about the bigger picture now. It's never too early to start that discussion with your kids.

Life for the Next Generation
Gen Alpha – the generation following Gen Z – includes all children born in or after 2010, which interestingly is the same year the iPad came into the world. By 2025, this generation will be more than two billion kids – which will be the largest generation in history. Scary, because that's just around the corner.

Their lives will undoubtedly be shaped by the pandemic just as much as, if not more than, the lives of millennials, Gen Z, and Gen X, who were forced to rethink jobs and education and travel. They're the kids who were home-schooled in lockdown and forced to wear masks to school while they were too young to really understand it. It goes without saying that they're heavily influenced by technology, world events, social media, and their peers, and they're inhabiting a very different world from the one we've known.

These kids have been exposed to new ways of working already as they watched their parents' careers change over the pandemic. Work will be very different for them, and they will see work from home and remote study as a normal way of life. They won't have one stable job for life. They're the kids who are going to have multiple careers and do lots of different things in life. They're also the generation that already care about social and environmental issues like climate change and social justice at a young age.

This generation was raised on screens, so we need to understand that it's very different from our upbringing. They had so much more screen time during the pandemic, with school and even catch-ups with friends over Zoom and FaceTime. They're growing up quickly and are consuming technology faster than any other generation.

Through this access to technology, they're exposed to so much in this world, with access to more information than any generation before it. There will be a shift in what they define as aspirational in the future. Kids of this generation are being increasingly exposed to role models who are trailblazers, entrepreneurs, and household celebrities, many of whom are just kids themselves.

We're at a really pivotal point in history now. Our economy is at a point of reinvention. We're in the middle of an economic paradigm shift, and things are looking quite different from how it's been in the past. A lot has changed even in the last few years. Successful reinvention of our economy will rest on creating significantly better financial understanding among the next generations through education to enable smart, long-term financial decision-making.

This is an opportunity of reinvention—of our mindset, of our careers, and of our next economic chapter. The future depends on what we teach our kids about money.

THE INTERGENERATIONAL
TRANSFER OF WEALTH

Speaking of the next generation of kids, we're in the middle of the biggest intergenerational wealth transfer in history, and we need to get talking about it.

Opens on Jane's parents, sitting in their kitchen having tea and toast together at breakfast.

BOB — Did you hear that woman on the TV yesterday? She said baby boomers are handing over $3.5 trillion to the next generation. We've been the richest generation ever. Ha! More like the hardest working.

CATH — Three trillion. How much even is that?

BOB — A bloody lot of money. And I bet a lot of 'em will blow it.

CATH — Well, that's not the first thing I think about. You're so negative, Bob.

BOB — Negative? Know the facts, woman! That woman said research showed that 70 percent of people who get an inheritance blow it. Science, Cath, science.

CATH — Probably more research than science but okay, Bob. At least we can leave Jane the house.

$\longrightarrow$

BOB	Yes, and that will be worth a pretty penny. Old Reg next door just got 2.3 million for his shack, and our block is bigger.
CATH	Oh, and their garden is terrible. Those old-lady roses. Please!
BOB	We should get the house valued and find out what it could be worth for our Janey.
CATH	When we go, of course. Which hopefully is a while away yet.
BOB	Yes, I suppose so. Jane did say she wanted us to see that friend of hers. The financial planner.
CATH	Well, maybe we should. It would be good.
BOB	I don't trust 90 percent of these so-called experts. But it can't hurt to check him out.
CATH	I'll ring Jane and let her know.

Making the Right Windfall Decisions

Bob's comment about blowing it wasn't wrong. If 70 percent of us did blow it up the wall with holidays and cars, then we would have a boom on travel and motor vehicles for ten or so years, and then we'd be back to where we were before, but a decade down the track. This money needs to be invested wisely. In my book, the characters lucked out having Ben as an old school friend. He came along and gave each of them some damn good financial advice (for a fee of course), which helped each of them make crucial decisions about their future.

Bob and Cath were advised to sell their large home, buy a retirement unit, and allow Jane to invest in her super with the rest. That way they could be sure she had her own nest egg when she turned sixty-five. They might not be around in twenty years, but their gift of a comfortable retirement income gave Jane a happy last third of her life. What a legacy.

Not all advice was the same from Ben, but each time, he was considering what each of them needed to give them security into the future as well.

Jasper and his mum Isobel looking at units in the same street as hers.

JASPER — I dunno, Mum. Are you sure you want me living in the same street? Feels a bit weird.

ISOBEL — Weird? What's weird about wanting to be close to my only son?

JASPER — I guess, but why move out from your place at all, since we are on the same street?

ISOBEL — So you have a chance of having a normal life. Finding a wife. Being happy.

JASPER — Yeah, well you never know, Ma. I am enjoying knowing Jane again.

ISOBEL — She is a lovely woman, that's for sure. But she does have two kids. Are you ready for that?

JASPER — I like kids. Sort of. I think she is the kind of woman it would be worth it for.

$\longrightarrow$

ISOBEL	Hmm, well, okay. I have never heard you be this serious before, so that's a good thing.
JASPER	**This unit has a crappy bathroom, Mum. There's no bath. And the tiles are pink.**
ISOBEL	It's in your price range, so suck it up.
JASPER	**Thanks. Ben did say this money might be better in my super, you know. And on studying.**
ISOBEL	I want to know you have a roof over your head. You can't blow that.
JASPER	**Thanks Mum, as always, for the vote of confidence.**

While Ben gave some sound advice around investing for Jasper in the future, and funding his career change study as a PE teacher, Isobel knew her son. She believed if the money wasn't spent on a property, he would blow it. Little did she know he would marry five years later and lose it in a divorce. By insisting on bricks and mortar, she actually took away the chance of Jasper having a well-funded retirement. But how was she to know? Bricks and mortar always worked for their generation. Safe as houses was what she knew. And she had long passed away by the time Jasper retired.

Talking with Your Kids about Inheritance

Inheritance is one of the most important discussions we can have with our kids, and it can be an emotional one. It has the potential to hugely impact their life if they use the money wisely. It can be a very beautiful conversation that gets them thinking about the bigger picture and family legacy. For some kids, they may have never even thought about this. For others, maybe they have thought about it and have never known how to bring it up.

YOU	We have been lucky the way real estate prices have gone up. We will be leaving you kids a good legacy. This house is worth a fair bit now. That makes us both very happy.
YOUR KID	I hate thinking about you dying, let's not talk about it.
YOU	Well, it's not so much about dying, but about what we have achieved, and what we will be able to leave for you all to have a better life.
YOUR KID	Well, that won't be for ages, I hate thinking about it.
YOU	I would be so happy to know you and your brothers have a buffer. We would love you to have a deposit each for your own home.
YOUR KID	How would that work?
YOU	We will make you executor of our will. When we pass on, the house will be sold and split three ways equally.
YOUR KID	I may not want a mortgage.
YOU	At least understand how much the bank would lend you.
YOUR KID	Okay, if it makes you happy.

$\longrightarrow$

YOU

> Yes, I'm happy thinking you will have security. We are setting up a meeting with you and your brothers next month to start going over it all. We would rather have it all out in the open when it comes to talking about money.

Note that in most of the dialogue I assign you, my reader, I leave the endings very "loose." What's going to happen next, you may wonder? And that's the beauty of it. Because what happens next is up to you. You may be in this situation or one so different that it's hard to compare. But reality, what I am saying is that starting money conversations is a long-term behavioural change in you. In time it will become that way with those around you too. Via your leadership. Any big change needs a champion and a believer. In your life, that has be you.

And if you're not planning on leaving an inheritance to your kids that is financial, then how are you defining your legacy? Your love for your children and your loyalty to your family extends far beyond money. Perhaps your caring for your grandchildren allows your kids to make money. Well, that's you investing in your kids. Without you it would be childcare, and that's not cheap. So it can come back to money in a different way, to celebrate and to appreciate. Your contribution is so valuable. So essential for your own kids and their families to have stability and thrive in an uncertain time. Please read this book in the spirit of understanding and valuing your own contribution, for you as much as those around you. There are billions around the globe who undertake service to others as their role in life.

> **NOT EVERYONE HAS TO BE ABOUT LEAVING MONEY. EVERYONE LEAVES A LEGACY. TAKE THIS OPPORTUNITY TO UNDERSTAND YOURS. I WANT THAT FOR YOU.**

Initiating the Inheritance Conversation

Here's what happens when I talk about inheritance with all different kinds of people. When you are me, there is no way some question about money won't come up at some point, and I have been told I like a chat. In any grouping, from a family BBQ to the ladies' bathroom at a conference, I seem to connect with people who have fascinating pasts and insights. As soon as people know what I do, they tend to loosen right up about their particular story. I love it. It may be the best part of what I do.

I have been known to make friends in bathrooms and restaurants, and also to take random selfies with people who told me a great story. I love getting personal. It genuinely fascinates me how courageous people are. How strong, how enduring. I have heard some incredibly heartbreaking stories from women and men (see, not only making friends in the ladies' bathroom) about money and the impact on their lives. But when I ask them about inheritance, it goes something like this.

ME So that was a great story about how you landed your first job. You are quite the go-getter. Now, tell me, have you spoken to your parents about an inheritance? Is that on the cards for you?

MILLENNIAL I CALL MIA Inheritance? Oh, no. I would never ask them about that. It would be considered very rude in my family. *(in bathroom at a leadership conference)*

ME Why?

MIA Because we would never speak about money. We have some, and I am sure Mum and Dad will leave me and my siblings something, but we won't know until they pass on. I don't even think about it.

ME Okay, you just told me you worked for sixty hours straight on a submission to get this job, but talking with your parents is a no-go zone.

MIA That's right.

ME Wow. That must be tough. You are missing out on such a big opportunity to create a tangible legacy in your family while your parents are still around.

MIA Really? How do you mean?

ME Your parents would probably love the opportunity to reflect on their life, their achievements and contribution. So often that only happens for people at their funeral, which I think kind of sucks, because wouldn't we all rather hear the good stuff while we are still here? That's what creating a legacy is all about. Starting the conversation. Not really talking about money straight up. That comes later.

MIA This sounds really good. How can I learn more?

ME Follow me on Insta. Or check out the free stuff on my website. Good luck!

MIA Thanks V, you are the best. *(Okay, so I added this, but I'm the writer...so, deal.)*

Most people find it damn rude to talk about money. With their parents or others, like grandparents, from whom inheritance would have a big financial impact on their lives. It could be, if you knew that confidence around getting an inheritance would allow you more freedom to live the life you really want. You might just have the confidence to start your own business, knowing you had capital. Or to finally take some time off work and travel. For others it might mean medical expenses could be covered, a mortgage could be paid, and a huge financial load will be lifted.

When you think about the joy an inheritance could bring to your life, or the lives of those around you, I see it as common sense to start talking about it. Start using your energy for positive thinking around the future and what it could mean for all of you.

It most likely is that your own adult children, if you have them, are avoiding this very conversation as we speak. Which is why I have developed this cheat sheet to help you on your way. But using these conversation starters and organising a dedicated occasion to launch the conversation, your inheritance strategy can come to life. And you can do your best to make sure your entire family gets the most from it for generations to come.

Suggested Conversation Starters

1. Schedule a catch-up with all of the loved ones that will be impacted, and put it in their diary. Whether it's a lunch, a zoom call, or a BBQ, think about what type of get-together is most in line with your family values, and do that. It's important to make sure no one is left out, so if someone is interstate or overseas, best to make it a virtual catch-up.

2. Set the ground rules. Make sure you tell everyone ahead of time what this event is about, and why you want to do it. If you catch people off-guard on the day, emotions are heightened, so it's vital to give people time to process what they are about to hear.

3. Go in with an agenda, and stick to it. Really think through what you all want to say, and don't stray from this. In the moment, it can be easy to change your words to protect or shelter loved ones, but it's important not to. Talk about what you want the legacy to be, and how the person wants to be remembered, as this will help loved ones understand the *why* and reasoning behind all decisions.

4. Give them the chance to ask questions, but not until you've finished. Once you've said everything you wanted to, open the floor to everyone else. It's natural for people to have reactions, but it's also

normal if people are still processing and don't know what to say. They can ask more questions at a later date.

5. Set up another meeting. This is perhaps the most important step. Everyone will need time to digest the information, and a few weeks or months later you can get everyone together to talk through more specific details. Getting everyone on the same page is crucial in avoiding conflicts down the track, and it gives people the chance to come to terms with choices while they have the opportunity to ask questions.

HAVE COURAGEOUS CONVERSATIONS WITH YOUR KIDS (AND GRANDKIDS)

Talking with your kids about money can be fun or emotionally charged. If they're younger, you could make a game of it and write questions on little pieces of paper and put them in a hat.

With your adult children, it's really about having an open discussion. Have a few key things you want to talk about, such as inheritance, their financial security, and what they want out of life. If that's too much, just start with one topic.

When it comes to the younger kids, it's about teaching them some money skills, understanding their money personalities, and trying to get them to develop good money habits early on. It's an opportunity to get to know them better and pass on some of your knowledge from all your years of experience.

Before you start, it might also be a good idea to take a moment to reflect on your own money beliefs and biases that might be rubbing off on your kids.

These questions are just a guide to get you started. You could also make your own up as you go!

Questions to Ask Yourself

- What are some beliefs you can recognise you're holding onto that are spilling out into your actions and words? How can you change this so your kids are exposed to something more positive?

- What can you learn about finances to help educate your kids more? Where can you find more help? (There is so much information online these days, and a lot of it is completely free. Start there.)

- How can you start to teach your kids about money?

- For the young kids, have you considered a reward system at home for doing chores or a way to help them save and put some money away? What can you do to give your kids a head start as early as possible?

- Have you talked to your kids about how having a bank account works, how to save money, and how to start thinking about budgeting their money? It might be an idea to open up a bank account for them and get them to see what it's like to manage their own money.

- Have you thought of introducing them to the world of investing?

- How can you talk to your kids about your legacy and their inheritance? What do you want them to know about what you want to leave them, and what you would like to see them do with that money?

Questions to Ask Little Kids

- What would you do with a million dollars?

- If you could have all the money in the world, how much would you want and why?

- What do you want to be when you grow up?

- How much do you really think it really costs to run a house?

- How much do you think your school fees cost?

- If we could have a family holiday every year, where would you want to go?

- What would you be willing to cut back on if we could have a family holiday every year?

- What do you really want to save up for?

- If you were going to buy shares in a company, what company would you choose?

- Are there any questions about money you want to ask me?

- Is there anything you don't understand about money?

- Do you know what compound interest is?

Questions to Ask Big Kids

- What do you really want in life, if you could do anything?

- If you had some money come your way, what would you want to do with it?

- Have you invested in the stock market or cryptocurrency?

- Do you have any debts?

- What is it you really care about? What are your main values?

- What could I do to help you get on top of your finances?

What did you get out of the conversation? Take a moment to reflect on what you said and any insights you got from each other. I hope you got a few laughs out of it and learned something new from each other!

Chapter 4

THE AWKWARD + UNAVOIDABLE CONVERSATION YOU NEED TO HAVE WITH YOUR PARENTS (AND SIBLINGS)

4

MONEY MATTERS:
THE PAST VS. THE PRESENT

There's no doubt about it. At some point in our relationship with our parents, things change. Hopefully, if we get enough time with our parents, we get to see them start to age. To slow down. At first it is almost unimaginable to see your strong, vital father get frail, or your feisty mother become so thin and slow. We start to see them wear thicker glasses, take more naps, and acknowledge the talk about their bowel habits and aching knees as well as the other ailments that they and those around them are experiencing.

But it also means that our relationship with caring for them and money changes too. We now can become our parents' carers more than their children.

Do you know your parents' retirement plan? Do you know their wishes? Have they ever broached where they would like to live when they are older? These are all topics that can be extremely scary and fraught with emotion for those going through it.

Opens to Karen on the phone to her mum, explaining how the internet connection could be reset on her iPad.

KAREN

Yep, Mum, I think you have it now. Glad I could be IT support again.

GLORIA

Thanks, love. I can't stand that damn thing.

RUSS

I know, Ma. But you love the photos of the kids I send on it.

GLORIA

That's true. I always take it to the club with me to show the others.

$\rightarrow$

KAREN   Nice. How's your friend Beryl doing? I know she was worried about her daughter last time we spoke.

GLORIA   Oh yes, she is having awful trouble with that horrible son-in-law she has. He's trying to make her sell the house so they can buy one big enough to fit them all and have Beryl in the small in-law accommodation out back.

KAREN   Oh, that's tough. Although it might be nice for Beryl to know her daughter is right there. Even if her husband is not Beryl's favourite.

GLORIA   Oh yes, I suppose so. She's very upset about it all. You know how emotional she is.

KAREN   Well, it must be a weird time of life, where you let go of your independence to an extent.

GLORIA   Yes, there's a lot of that going on with your father and me.

KAREN   What's your plan, Mum? What do you and Dad want to do?

GLORIA   Oh, I don't know. Moving seems like a lot of work. We will probably just die here.

KAREN   Really? Wouldn't you and Dad like to go to one of those nice retirement villages? They have separate homes still, but you get assistance, and meals and cleaning help. To be honest, it would be ideal for you. There's a lot of work for you both to keep the house up.

→

GLORIA	Yes, it is a lot of work. Your father fell off the back step last week, banged up his knee.
KAREN	I'm worried that will just get worse. I think it's worth looking into those places, Mum. At least see what they cost and get some advice. You own the house outright. You should have more than enough. I will start making some calls for you.
GLORIA	Your father and I don't want to use the money from the house on us. We want to give it to you and your brothers.
KAREN	Well, you deserve a great retirement too. Let's talk about this. I'll cook lunch next Sunday, and Russ will drive down and pick you both up. Nate needs practice driving anyway.
GLORIA	Lunch sounds lovely. I will bring a dessert. Tell Nate that Nana said he better be safe.
KAREN	I'm sure he will be on his best behaviour, Mum. Love you.
GLORIA	Love you too.

Unlearning Money Narratives

Baby boomers grew up in a time after World War II. They were taught how to be frugal, how to make money spin out and live within their means. But the world has changed so much that sometimes it's hard to get your parents seeing eye-to-eye with you when it comes to money today. But having money conversations with your parents is vital – especially as they age and you become an adult – because, the earlier you can have the conversation, the more strategic you can be in making financial decisions that benefit everyone. And this is probably the time when you will need to seek specialist advice.

Scene opens on Jane at the mall with her parents Bob and Cath.

BOB By god, that kid over there is screaming like a banshee. I'd give that one a good smack on the backside.

JANE Yeah, you aren't supposed to smack kids anymore, Dad. It scars them.

BOB Didn't scar you any. Or are you going to tell me you are scarred now?

JANE No, Dad, I am pretty good. It was different times than nowadays. Everyone got a smack back then.

CATH Yes, well, I would always get told that to spare the rod would spoil the child by my father.

BOB Now, let's find these new parkas for the girls so I can get out of here. What is on sale?

JANE I want to get them at the outdoor store, Dad. It's for their camp.

BOB They are twice the price there. Don't be ridiculous.

⟶

Vanessa Stoykov

JANE	Well, it's how I choose to spend my money, Dad. Lucky I earn it.
BOB	**Yes, well, I am only looking out for you, Janey. You know we want you to have money in the bank.**
JANE	Yes, Dad, I know. But how about you? What's your money situation looking like? I've never really asked you before, but my friend Ben, who is a financial planner, was talking about how it's good to know what your parents' plans are.
BOB	**Did he? Hmmm. Well, I'm not up to telling some stranger about our personal business.**
JANE	Well, you would be talking with me first. I would love to know what you are thinking and what you and Mum want.
CATH	That could be nice.

Taking a Trip Down Memory Lane

Jane is faced with the attitude of her parents that they don't "air their dirty laundry" with strangers. But she is smart enough to know that asking her dad to at least start the conversation about money and the future with her was a first step. Nobody can make big decision or life choices in a single conversation. Starting the conversation with your parents at various times without making a big deal of it, and agreeing to a future discussion, is a great start. It doesn't matter where you begin – it's talking about things that is the start of it all.

> **OPENING UP ABOUT MONEY WITH OUR PARENTS CAN FEEL CHALLENGING, AWKWARD, AND UNCOMFORTABLE, AND THAT IS WHY MANY PEOPLE HAVE NEVER HAD A CONVERSATION ABOUT MONEY WITH THEIR PARENTS.**

Maybe you're embarrassed to talk about it because you don't think you're good with money and you're afraid of their judgements. Maybe you grew up in a house where money was never discussed and so you don't feel like you can talk about it with your parents. Or perhaps you remember your parents fighting about money, so it's a topic you want to avoid because of the conflict that can arise.

Choosing a Financial Lane of Your Own

Jasper grew up watching his father work himself to death. And Jasper, when he was young, decided that he didn't want to be like his father. So he went too far the other way, to be as little like his dad as possible. He went from one job to the next with no passion or interest and not really caring what he did day to day. He would go out drinking with friends without a plan or any idea of what he was doing it for. He got to his forties and realised he didn't have anything to his name, was living with his mum, and his friends thought he was hopeless.

Jasper had to unlearn the subliminal belief he had developed, which was that hard work equated to an unhappy life. Although he didn't want to be a workaholic like his father, he still needed to find his passion and what he really wanted in life.

You don't have to work hard; you can work smart. You don't have to be like your father to earn money; you can find other avenues. As I've said, it's not about what you don't know about money, it's what you do know — how you grew up, how your beliefs shaped you, all the things in your past around money that have become bad habits. Most people need to stop and acknowledge what these are before they can actually move forward, change things, and build new goals and better habits.

Talking with Your Parents about Inheritance

A lot of people who receive an inheritance have never even had a conversation with their parents about money, let alone talk about what they intend their inheritance to be used for. When you think about it, this is really sad, because that money has been hard-earned, and parents may have had a wish for their legacy which they possibly never spoke about. That's why I want you to get talking about money and inheritance with your parents before it's too late.

While nobody likes to think about dying or of their loved ones passing away, it is really important to be prepared for the future and to know what's coming. It doesn't feel good to talk about anyone in the family dying, and it can bring up a lot of raw emotions. We need to get real and start having these conversations because avoiding them isn't going to do anyone any favours, especially when we're trying to plan ahead for the future.

If you know or think you'll be receiving an inheritance, you should definitely have a conversation with your parents about what they intend this money to be used for. I really encourage you to discuss with your parents your thoughts on how you might invest the money and what your future plans are. You want to make sure you're honouring your parents' wishes while using the money wisely. We should never assume we know what others want, and that goes for both sides. This is why it needs to be an open conversation.

This is an opportunity that shouldn't be wasted. It's a good idea to figure out how much you might inherit by talking openly about it with your parents. If they don't want to talk about it, ask them why. Maybe you will learn more about them in this process.

YOU
I know we've never talked about this before, but I was wondering about your legacy, and what you are planning on regarding inheritance.

YOUR PARENT
I'm glad you brought this up. I've been meaning to talk to you about it. There's a bit of money I've put aside for you and your siblings. I want to make sure it is split up evenly, so you all get a fair share. There's a decent amount of money there that you can use toward a house deposit or a mortgage.

YOU
That's so good to hear. Thank you. But what if I wanted to spend it on something else, like some other investments?

YOUR PARENT
Well, I hadn't thought of that. What do you have in mind?

YOU
I have been thinking about starting a stock market portfolio. I've been doing a lot of research and I just need some money to kickstart it. Would you be okay if I used some of this money toward that?

YOUR PARENT
Well, as long as it's not going to go down the drain. It sounds a bit risky. I never touched the stock market.

YOU
I've been doing a lot of research and I would speak to a financial planner to do it properly. There is some risk involved, but it can have even better returns than real estate.

$\longrightarrow$

> **YOUR PARENT** Well, how about I give you $10,000 of the money now so you can start this, and if it works then you can figure out for yourself what to do with the rest of the money. I just want to make sure that you don't waste it and that you'll have a place to live, so don't rule out buying a house one day, okay?
>
> **YOU** **Okay, thanks for your help and support. This is a huge helping hand for me! I'll make sure to use the money wisely.**

Intergenerational Money Matters

It's difficult to speak openly about money, but it's especially challenging to talk about it across generations. Talking about money has been taboo with older generations for a reason. But those reasons don't hold much weight nowadays.

It can also be an uncomfortable conversation with our parents because the conversation about mortality comes up. If we involve siblings, hidden conflicts can arise, and emotions can get the better of us too.

KAREN	I've asked Bruce and Ray over for lunch too, Mum. If we are going to talk about money and plans, they may as well be involved.
GLORIA	Oh, I would rather talk to you first. It always upsets your brothers thinking of anything happening to Dad or me.
KAREN	Well, you are their parents too, so they need be involved. I am sure they will handle it. They are grown men.
GLORIA	Your father is going to hate this. I don't know how well it will go.
KAREN	Well, I think it will be good for our family. Bring us together. Get the boys back involved again, Mum. I know they don't call much.
GLORIA	Well, they are always busy at work. We understand that. But, yes, I guess it would be good to see them and talk about it.

The Intention of Legacy

Have you discussed with your parents what they do and don't want their money to be used for if they're handing you an inheritance? Have you considered what you want to do with your inheritance and talked to them about it?

THE FIRST QUESTION SHOULD ALWAYS BE: WHAT IS YOUR INTENTION IN GIVING THIS GIFT?

As a receiver of an inheritance, you need to consider what your parents' intention is and what they want their legacy to represent. Is it to give your family security, a home, an education, or to give you a head start?

The more intentional you are about how you use your inheritance, and make a long-term plan for your future, the more that wealth transfer will lead to creating an investment in the future that will keep giving for generations to come. And the more you understand from your parents about what their intention for the money is for you, the wiser you'll be when it comes to using it.

Can you take this opportunity to think deeply about what you really want from your life and how this money could help? What most parents want is to give future generations a happier, easier life than they had. They want you to feel secure and they want you to be happy.

Remembering the Dream
When presented with the potential of receiving an inheritance, you find yourself with opportunity at your fingertips. With inheritance, you can finally afford to make some things come true.

In Chapter 1, we talked about figuring out what it is that you really want in your life, and in Chapter 2, we discussed how this needs to work with your partner (if this is applicable to you). I encourage you to go back to imagining that dream life for yourself. Because here's the thing, with an inheritance it becomes a lot easier to make that a reality. It's a blessing and an opportunity. This is something to be really excited about. I'm excited for you.

Go back to remembering what it is you really want in life. It could be travelling, living in a different city, going back to study, starting a business, buying a family home, living debt-free and mortgage-free, moving to the country or the city, sending your kids to a top-notch school or being able to pay for their university fees, or having the option to go all in and start working for yourself. Whatever it is, it needs to be about what brings you joy and align with your life values.

> **START BY THINKING ABOUT HOW YOUR INHERITANCE CAN HELP YOU LIVE YOUR DREAM LIFE—FOR THE LONG TERM. THEN GET TALKING ABOUT IT.**

You need to think about what it is you want for your life and how this money is going to help you get that. If you intend to use this money to help you start a business, you should probably have a conversation with your parents about it first to make sure they are happy for their money to go toward this, because they might have a different idea. You might never agree. But doesn't it feel great to have meaningful conversations with people you love?

You might be thinking of passing the wealth on to a charity you're passionate about. And that can be a beautiful thing to do, especially if you don't really need the money yourself. I think the age of giving is really going to grow in this wealth transfer. My hope is that philanthropy will move out of being a wealthy person's domain, to the everyday person who has been given a windfall and wants to make a difference.

> **AN INHERITANCE GIVES YOU A HUGE BOOST IN THE RIGHT DIRECTION, BUT YOU'VE GOT TO BE CLEAR ON WHAT THAT DIRECTION IS.**

Think about Your Own Legacy

Whatever inheritance you're getting is going to impact your own kids, if you have them or want them some day. If you've got kids, chances are your parents are thinking about them in the picture too. Your parents probably want to take into consideration establishing their grandchildren's future.

While your parents might leave an inheritance directly to the grandkids, your money is also likely going to be passed down to your own kids someday. When you're thinking of what you do with the money now, you will want to consider your kids down the line too.

Think about what you want to leave behind when you're gone, while living your life with purpose and being true to your values.

Could you give to make the world a better place? Think about what difference you would like to make from a social or environmental perspective. Have you thought about philanthropy? Can you give some of your windfall to make the world a better place?

Rather than just manage your finances, can you help support a cause that is close to your own heart and give? Whether it would be for animals, children, the elderly, or the planet, there are so many fantastic causes out there that desperately need financial support.

CHANGING TIMES AND REVERSED ROLES

Bridging the Financial Gap

Self-made baby boomers worked hard for their money and built their wealth on grit. It was about persistence, hard work, and a regular paycheck to save steadily over a long time. Eventually it paid off, and they were able to buy the family home they wanted, and hopefully they've been able to enjoy their retirement while being able to leave a legacy for their kids.

Many of those who built their wealth from scratch remember what it's like to have nothing. But they're looking at a generation whose spending habits are quite different from theirs. And this is at a time when it's all too easy to transfer a lot of money online in a matter of seconds.

If I'm honest, they're probably a bit anxious about spending their hard-earned money in a new world, especially considering all that's going on in the world right now and how quickly things have changed. Not only are we in the midst of a pandemic, but everything is run online these days. It's a really different world from the one they've known.

As our parents age, the conversation needs to be had about what's going to happen as they get too old to look after themselves independently. Unfortunately, many of us wait until it's far too late before approaching this conversation. It's better to start the conversation before the time comes, so you know what your parents would want. It will also help to get a start on understanding aged care, which can be a bigger process than you expect, depending on where you live.

Tying Up Loose Ends with a Financial Adviser
I can't stress this enough. Getting professional advice is invaluable when you are considering aged care. There's a myriad of things to consider, and a financial planner will help you understand the welfare system, aged care costs, and what it means for any assets your parents have. Aged care is not cheap, and it is often said that the last ten years of our lives are the most expensive. Being prepared and understanding the implications will also help you talk to your parents in a way that gives them and your siblings all the facts.

It's equally important for your parents to consult a financial planner if they're leaving an inheritance or planning their final move for aged care. There are many ways to structure a legacy that works for each individual you are leaving for. You can make sure your wishes and the timing of money goes how you want it to when making a trust, a legal way to make sure the legacy is used the right way. Getting this peace of mind is only possible when you consult a professional, who knows the tax system and the laws because it's their job.

While many people don't want to pay for advice, if you have anything worth leaving, it is worth getting the right advice on how to maximise it. It is money you won't regret spending. And you might find that having a planner involved in discussions with your parents or your children can be a good buffer to defuse difficult conversations. If it is hard to talk about money, a planner can clearly present the money situation as it is, without the emotion attached.

It's also a good idea to sort out your will, no matter how much you have, or how old you are. The only way to ensure your legacy, including insurance, is used the way you want is by having a will, a plan, and conversations with loved ones well before anything happens.

Sometimes getting a professional involved is the best way to make sure you get the right outcome.

HAVE A COURAGEOUS CONVERSATION WITH YOUR PARENTS (AND SIBLINGS)

Having a conversation with your parents about money can be fire-fuelled. It can also be a great opportunity to get to know each other as adults, with better insight into the realities of life. And of course your siblings may not agree with you on the best way to have this conversation or take care of your parents. So the earlier you start this conversation with them too, the better it will be. There are many ways you want bring it up. Sometimes asking them what their fears are will be a good trigger to start a money conversation.

YOU

Mum, Dad, what's your biggest fear about what will happen to your legacy money when you die?

YOUR PARENT

In all honesty, I'm a bit worried you or your partner will blow it all. I worked hard for that money, you know, and I wouldn't want you to waste it on silly things.

YOU

I wouldn't want to blow it either, Dad, and I know you sacrificed a lot to give us the life we have. What would make you happy and proud with the legacy you have created?

YOUR PARENT

I'd want you to have a nice home and a healthy, happy family and enjoy a holiday once in a while. Really, I just want to see you happy. But I want you to be sensible too. The good things in life are the simple things. Work hard while you can, and enjoy the little things in life.

YOU

I want that too, Dad. How do you want to be remembered when you're gone?

YOUR PARENT

I want to be remembered as a dad that gave you a good life and did my best to help you out. I don't want you to think of me as a grumpy old man. I know I can be sometimes, but we had a lot of fun when you were younger. Those family trips in the country when you were little kids were the best times.

$\longrightarrow$

> **YOU**   I know, Dad, I remember, and I appreciate everything you've done for us. We have had a good upbringing because of you and Mum. Maybe we can do another family trip like that soon. I'm really glad we had this chat.

Suggested Conversation Starters

Talking with your aging parents about money:

- What's your biggest fear about getting older?

- What would you like to happen if you lose your ability to live independently?

- What has been your biggest lesson with money?

- How can I help you prepare for what's ahead?

- What is it you really want for me for the future?

- What do you think I should and shouldn't do with my money and my inheritance?

- How do you want to split an inheritance with our siblings?

- How much am I likely to inherit?

- If you were in my shoes, what would you do?

- How do you want to be remembered?

- What do you think our family legacy is?

- What's your money story that you picked up from childhood?

- What are some money habits you've got to unlearn from your past that you might have picked up from your parents or the way you grew up?

- What do you really want in life and how can an inheritance help you get there?

- How can your parents help you live the life you really want?

- What does freedom and financial prosperity mean to you?

- What would your financial picture look like if you were financially free?

- What steps can you take to help make that a reality? How can your parents help you get there?

- What did your parents teach you about money and what did they do to help you on your way?

Cherish Your Aging Parents

Having these conversations with your aging parents can stir up quite the emotion. Remember that life is short. Tell the people you love how much you care for and appreciate them. Focus on the time together, and be grateful for all that you have, even if it isn't perfect. We don't know what's ahead, but these are times to treasure. Of course, money is important, but love and communication are the most important of all.

Having these conversations with family can do wonders to bring people closer together, even if you don't always agree with everyone. I wish nothing but the best for you and your family as you navigate these somewhat difficult conversations that need to be had.

Chapter 5

THE RAW + HONEST CONVERSATION YOU NEED TO HAVE WITH YOUR FINANCIAL ADVISER

5

> **WE AVOID CONVERSATIONS ABOUT MONEY WITH THOSE CLOSEST TO US FOR A LONG TIME, BUT MANY OF US LEAVE CONSULTING A PROFESSIONAL UNTIL IT'S TOO LATE.**

If you've made it this far, congratulations! Getting real about your finances and having candid conversations about money with those closest to you is not easy. But by opening up about money and getting more comfortable talking about it, you're breaking down the stigma and the barriers that have been holding you back.

Up until this point, you've done the groundwork by asking yourself all the important questions and talking openly about money with the important people in your life. You've probably had some financial flashpoints along the way that've got you figuring out what's important to you and what you want to work toward. Now it's about creating a financial plan that aligns with the life you want and taking action to get you there. That's where good financial advice comes in.

While you've been assessing your money situation, you've probably identified some pain points where you could probably do with some help. Managing money and understanding tax implications can be confusing, and you generally need a bit of guidance to get moving in the right direction. Whether it's managing your own money, shared finances with your partner, or being equipped to talk to your parents or kids about estate planning, speaking to a financial adviser can really help.

All sorts of emotions can crop up when we open up about finances with our partner, parents, and kids, but it's also difficult to talk about your financial situation with a professional. Whether you're worried about feeling judged by someone for your money decisions or you're concerned about how much it's going to cost to get financial advice, there's a reason why you haven't taken the step yet. Maybe you don't really believe you can change your money situation, so you don't think it would be worth the effort, or perhaps you just don't think you can trust anyone else with your personal finances. You might think you're not earning enough money to warrant seeing an adviser, or maybe you don't think you're ready to invest your money.

Too many people think seeing a financial adviser is out of their league. But I believe everyone should have access to the wealth of knowledge and guidance that an adviser can provide. Everyone, no matter their financial situation or their background, deserves to enjoy financial freedom and security, which can be accessed through the advice of an expert. In the same way that we have a doctor to keep our health in order, a financial expert will keep you on top of your financial health.

Some of the best things in life are things that money can't buy. Sunsets, time with family, laughs with friends, an afternoon at the beach. But the irony is that we need to be financially stable and secure to have the freedom to enjoy these free things. (And a cocktail in hand would be nice too!) The good life comes at a cost, but all it takes is putting a few solid practices in place. You can do that with some practical guidance from the people who know their stuff when it comes to money. Even if it takes a little bit of sacrifice in the short term, you can have money and enjoy your life at the same time. Really, the two go hand in hand.

Many of us resist seeking advice, and we often decide to manage our financial affairs ourselves. A lot of people make the mistake of thinking that financial advice is just for the wealthy. But financial advice can help you plan for things as simple as a holiday or something as complex as buying a property, or retiring comfortably.

Managing your money is such an important part of managing life. Seeing a financial adviser should not be reserved only for the rich, because access to this kind of specialist knowledge is incredibly valuable and it can really change your life.

FINANCIAL ADVISER
READINESS

Are you ready for a financial adviser? If you're reading this book, and have gotten this far, you must be ready to straighten out your finances once and for all. But I know that seeking financial advice can feel like a really big step for many people, especially if you haven't done it before (except maybe getting an accountant to do your tax which isn't quite the same thing).

You may or may not be ready for professional advice yet and that's okay. You've got to look at your own personal situation and assess what's right for you right now. Just the fact that you've started to identify some gaps and learn about money management and wealth creation is a great first step. If you're not ready yet, you might come back to this part later. Being vulnerable with yourself and your family and friends about your money situation and fears is the first big step to being able to improve your money story. Getting a professional is the next step if you decide it's right for you.

FINANCIAL ADVISER
BENEFITS

Like you would see a counsellor to get through some personal issues, a financial adviser is there to help you straighten out a hugely important part of life – your finances.

Developing real financial literacy and building your financial confidence is truly life-changing. I wish everyone had access to good financial advice, because all too often I see people not really knowing the best way to prepare for the future – because they didn't know how to plan properly and invest their money with a long-term view.

> I WHOLEHEARTEDLY BELIEVE IN THE POWER OF GREAT FINANCIAL ADVICE. IT IS AN ABSOLUTE GAME-CHANGER, AND WE ALL NEED IT NOW MORE THAN EVER.

The sooner you start planning, the sooner you can build the life you want, and live with better peace of mind. A financial planner has the technical expertise to develop the right strategy for you. They will know the latest legislative changes and ensure you feel financially informed and confident about your future.

If you're trying to make some changes to your financial future and put some good practices in place, it helps to involve an expert to help you navigate those important decisions. If you're ready to invest your money, if you're handling an inheritance, if you want to make a plan for your retirement, or if you're trying to create a life plan, whether it's on your own or together with your partner or even if you want to help your kids create a plan for their future, it's helpful to talk to a third party who can give you sound advice – particularly someone who has seen situations like yours over and over again.

People seek financial advice at different life stages. A young professional or couple might want to preserve the capital they're saving and investing, while a retiree is thinking about making sure they have enough to live on in retirement while being able to leave a legacy for the next generation. So, it's really about tailoring your needs to your goals.

Life changes, and what you do with your money changes at different stages of life, so you need to keep adapting your financial advice too. Whether you're young and in debt from university or college fees or you have made mistakes with money and you're wondering if you're ever going to get to financial security, there are experts in financial services who can absolutely help you out.

Navigating through a financial change requires sound advice, accountability, and perseverance. But having an adviser set things up for you will make the hard bits automated and simple so you don't need to think about it too much.

FINANCIAL ADVISING FLEXIBILITY

Almost two million Australians have seen a financial planner or adviser, and almost 40 percent of Americans work with a financial adviser. While some people keep a financial adviser for life, some switch for many reasons. It could be because their adviser lacked good communication or made some poor choices with stocks. Maybe they gave some bad advice, or maybe they just didn't feel a connection with their adviser.

If you're nodding your head in agreement here and you're not happy with your financial adviser, you can consider transferring to another. But it's important to check to see if there is any red tape involved with switching before you do anything. Read the fine print in the terms and conditions of your contract. Most of the time you simply have to send a signed letter to your adviser to terminate the contract. Before you say goodbye, make sure you collect your investment records too. Your new adviser might be able and willing to manage this for you and handle any paperwork for your transfer, which makes things easier for you.

If you've tried an adviser before and it didn't quite work, I encourage you to keep looking to find someone who is a good fit for you. Things change over your life, and where you may not have been ready before, you just might be now.

THE ROLE OF A
FINANCIAL ADVISER

The financial world is a maze of rules, products, and opinions on how to best manage money. If there's something you don't understand in the world of finance, you're not alone.

An adviser can give you insights into all you need to know when it comes to managing your finances — the ins and outs of tax, different investment options, how to distribute your money, how to save, and how to reduce debt. They will also ensure you have a retirement savings plan that will be not only enough, but more than enough, to live a good life in retirement.

Many people feel like they have no one to talk to about money. Having a financial adviser is like having someone to spill all your financial worries to and have them help you create solutions. An adviser will help look at your financial plan holistically and get you set up in the right direction.

Financial planning is about developing strategies to help you manage your financial affairs and meet your life goals. If you could achieve your financial goals by simply putting money away in the bank, you wouldn't need a financial plan. Unfortunately, life is a little more complex — it's hard to understand the intricacies of investment, taxation, and ever-changing rules and regulations, so you need professional help.

There are different levels of advice for different people, so it's a matter of finding what works for you. Just like finding the right nutritional plan for you, the same goes for financial advice. It's a tailored approach to your money plan that is a part of your broader life plan.

TRUSTING FINANCIAL ADVISERS

Yes, I know some of you just don't trust financial advisers because of something you've heard or read about. Maybe you aren't willing to open up your personal finances to anyone else, even with a professional expert in the field, because you're just not sure who you can trust with your money.

Financial advisers haven't always had a good rap. There have been some bad apples that have given the bunch a bad name. But like in any industry, there are some good (and great) financial advisers out there, but there are also some below-average ones. When it comes to getting good financial advice, it's really important that you find someone you trust.

A lot of people don't have their financial advice needs met because they are sceptical of the industry or don't know who to trust with their hard-earned cash, not because there aren't good people out there to help them. Missing out on good financial advice is unfortunate if you're held back because some people have been burnt in the past.

I've dealt with enough financial advisers in my time to know what to look for. I know there are thousands of incredible (and credible) advisers who are good at what they do. By working with them over the years I've seen how many of them genuinely care and want to help people and how incredibly smart they are when it comes to managing money.

But of course, it's important to find a financial adviser that you can trust and someone who listens to you about what you want out of life, what your values are, what your goals are, and what you're striving toward long-term. Financial advisers who want to have a long-term relationship with you and care about your personal goals tend to be the ones you can trust.

Financial planning is a specialist profession, and you should make sure that you're getting advice from a professional financial planner who is properly licensed and qualified.

Ten Questions to Ask a Financial Adviser

1. How long have you been a financial adviser?

2. Are you a member of the Financial Planning Association?

3. What academic and professional qualifications do you hold?

4. Are you a certified financial planning professional?

5. How do you charge for your services?

6. What's your specialty that you can offer advice on?

7. Who ultimately owns your practice?

8. What type of clients do you work with best?

9. What sort of clients do you typically see?

10. How often would we see each other?

Traits of a Good Financial Adviser

At the baseline, a good financial adviser will help you achieve your financial goals at any life stage and with any financial issue, from budgeting, to buying a house, to your retirement savings. There are a lot of financial advisers out there, so how do you know which one is actually right for you? Here are a few key things to look out for.

They will have your best interests at heart. Sure, a financial adviser is going to make some money from having you as a client because that is their business, but they should also have an interest in getting you ahead in life financially. Trust me, advisers like this definitely exist! Advisers that act as fiduciaries or trustees (who act on a client's behalf with a duty of trust) are a safe option, as they are required by law to act in the best interest of their clients.

They will also keep up-to-date with what's happening in the industry. A good financial adviser will know the latest when it comes to laws, tax codes, products, and ways to invest. If they keep up to date with what's happening, they'll have more knowledge to offer you the right advice.

They'll give you a clear direction about what will work for you. It can be overwhelming when you're confronted with lots of options and ways to invest. But a good adviser will help narrow down all the options for you and give you recommendations based on your individual needs to help make your investment decisions easier.

GETTING STARTED WITH FINANCIAL ADVISING

Financial Advising Affordability

If you want good financial advice, it of course does not come for free. Anything worthwhile will generally have a price tag attached. If you believe a financial adviser can help guide you to make positive choices with your finances, the benefits will no doubt outweigh the costs. This is an investment in your potential, so it's worth it if you are set on growing your wealth and living a financially healthy and prosperous life.

The question should not be can you afford it; it should be, can you afford not to?

We don't really question the money we spend when we go see the doctor or pay for our gym membership; the same should go for financial advice. Your financial health and well-being are just as important as your general health and well-being. Actually, your finances and your general health and stress levels are absolutely linked. The less stressed you are about money and the more financial freedom you have, the more likely you can look after yourself and your health.

Research shows that people who consult a financial planner feel happier and more positive about their financial well-being, and more optimistic about the future, than those who don't. That's because a financial planner will help you stay on track of your short-term goals, and the longer-term goals too.

It shouldn't be a question to spend money getting help with your finances if it's going to help you feel less stressed and happier. Why wouldn't you put the same level of investment into your money as your health?

Financial Advising Fees

It's important to be aware of the various fee structures because not all financial advisers charge in the same way.

Retainers are popular, which is where you pay a flat rate of, say, three hundred dollars a month or three to five thousand dollars a year or more for their ongoing service. With a retainer model, an adviser might usually charge a client an initial fee to build the financial plan, and once the plan is created, you would have access to the adviser whenever you need advice in exchange for the monthly or annual fee. The service fee they charge will depend on how complex your plan is.

In Australia, advisers must charge a fee for service, which means they won't get a commission on the products they offer you, but instead they'll get their revenue from the fees they charge you for their advice. This is the best way to make sure you're getting unbiased financial advice that's in your best interest, rather than going with a commission-based adviser who is making money from selling you products. It's really about transparency.

Many people don't think about getting financial advice because they simply don't think they fit into the pool of people who can afford it. But financial advice isn't just for people who are wealthy. Getting wealthy starts with getting good financial advice. It's a bit of a chicken-and-egg situation.

But here's the thing. You don't actually need to spend loads of money for financial advice. Ask your pension (superannuation) fund if they give advice to members. There are a number of ways to access help, including financial hotlines designed to help people having trouble find the right resources. What you need to do is be prepared to do a little of your own research.

If you're in debt or don't have any savings, you need more help than anyone to get yourself on your feet and grow your wealth. But if you think you can't afford an adviser yet because of your current financial situation, there are plenty of other resources out there. I am often amazed at how many great (free) resources are out there.

There are also government-backed organisations and financial counsellors who can help you get the advice you need to get you back on your feet. It's worth exploring the national debt helpline, free government resources (such as the Moneysmart website in Australia), and independent financial advisers' associations that can point you in the right direction.

There are also a growing number of low-cost online short courses you can take to teach you how to invest in the share market, how to create a budget spreadsheet, and how to save and pay down debt. You can never have too much financial education. Pace yourself, but keep learning.

Talking Points for Your Financial Adviser
Before you see a financial adviser, you'll want to
decide what you want to get out of it, which depends
on your stage of life, how much money you have, and
what you're trying to achieve.

You should be able to be brutally honest with your
financial adviser. Don't tell them what you think they
want to hear. Open up about your shortcomings and
what you really need help with. Tell them everything.
The more honest you are, the better off you'll be.

When discussing your finances and future
plans with your adviser, here's what should be on
the agenda:

- Your retirement plan

- Your five-, ten-, or twenty-year life plan

- Estate planning and your will

- A savings plan and debt reduction strategy

- An investment strategy

- How you can balance your cash flow
  and expenses

- Your financial goals

- How they'll manage your money

Sharing Openly with Your Financial Adviser
Some people are genuinely uncomfortable about
sharing their inner financial woes or wins to a stranger,
even if they are talking with a professional. Just as
there can be shame and pride attached to talking
about money with those closest to us, we can also
feel these emotions and others when we share our
personal finances with an expert.

There is really no need for you to feel ashamed
about where you are at with your finances now or

be too proud to seek help. Feeling like you're "bad with money" is just your mindset talking, and you can change that. You'll get more confident when you have a plan and start to see positive outcomes come out of the changes you make. Taking the step to seek advice is something that takes courage.

It's important to get really clear with your adviser on what their plan is when it comes to managing your wealth and your ongoing relationship. How often will you meet? What is their approach and strategy? What information will they provide you, and how often? How will they monitor and manage your investments? Will they consult you on their decisions? What commissions will they receive on the products they recommend to you? You should also discuss any terms for ending the contract with them too, if it ever came to this.

YOU

I really need to sort out my finances! I've been working for years, and I want to be able to buy a house and have enough for retirement, but I feel like I'm not getting anywhere. I have no savings!

ADVISER

You've come to the right place, and you're not the first person to tell me this! Let's start by looking at your cash flow, which are your incomings and outgoings. Then we can look at how much we can automate into savings and investments which will contribute to those long-term goals like a house. We'll also make sure you're contributing enough to your pension every year so you can afford the retirement you want. If you have any debt, we'll make a plan to clear that or at least work toward reducing it.

$\longrightarrow$

> **YOU**   I also want to enjoy my life now and be able to go on a holiday every year.
>
> **ADVISER**   That's fine! This is what life is about too. We can make sure you put away enough of your salary to spend on the fun things in life too. Let's start with your baseline expenses and see if there's anything you can cut down on, so you can keep some money for your annual holiday and enjoying your life while putting a percentage away for those long-term goals. It's all about distributing your money in the right way.

GETTING STARTED WITH INVESTING

I have had lots of conversations with financial experts about how to build wealth, and what it comes down to is learning to become a good investor. A lot of financially savvy people are living good lives because they've invested.

Increasing your savings and investing that money is the real way to financial success. Of course, those investments need to be different, or diversified, so that all your eggs aren't in one basket. For those who are business owners, often the biggest asset in the family is the business. I have seen fortunes changing very quickly, and it's important to remember to get money out of your business to invest in other areas where the risk is not so attached to you. Another great reason to talk to an adviser!

If you haven't started yet and have absolutely no savings or investments, there is no better time to start than right now. You can be late to the party and still find a way to get ahead. Yes, the power of compounding means that you are better off starting earlier, but you can only start from where you are now. So starting later is better than not starting at all.

Good financial planning involves thinking about the bigger picture – from considering the life you want to live to how you want to help others, whether it's passing on a legacy or being able to donate money to charity. Think about the life you want to live and what you want to be remembered for.

Seeing a financial adviser will help you create a plan that works for you. With a plan, you have a target, and you know the steps you need to take to get there. It's going to take some commitment up front, but when you follow a formula and have a plan, it's like riding a bike after a while – you get better at it. Just like a muscle, the more you use it, the stronger (and easier) It gets.

Set Realistic Goals
To have a solid plan, you need to get really clear on your goals. We all have different goals. Some of you may be saving for your first home, while others may want to set money aside for their kids' education, or maybe it's being able to travel. Maybe you want to have enough to enjoy a comfortable retirement.

Your investment goals are like following a map when going on a road trip. Even though you may know roughly how to get to your destination, you will still get there more quickly and with fewer detours, if you use a map.

A financial adviser will really help you calculate what you need to do to get there. That's their job. Whether it's trying to figure out when you can retire or how to pay off your debts or how to afford your mortgage, it's an adviser's job to run those figures for you and give you a realistic idea of what you need to do. Putting your trust in an expert, when you have a clear goal, will help you build a money machine that will set you free.

Don't underestimate the power of making the right decisions based around your goals. Just because you can't see the thing you want yet, doesn't mean it isn't on the horizon. Have a goal, have a plan to get there, get the help you need to guide you in the right direction and make the right choices, and then consistently work at it. It will come sooner than you may think.

> WHEN YOU START TO BELIEVE YOU CAN HAVE A DIFFERENT LIFE—AND A DIFFERENT FINANCIAL SITUATION— THAT'S WHEN YOU CAN START WORKING TOWARD A PLAN.

Wealth-Building Requires Time and Patience

As someone who has spent more than twenty-five years educating people about the intricate world of money and finance alongside experts in the field, I have found time and time again that it comes down to limiting thoughts and beliefs as the big reasons for people not getting the financial outcomes they want and deserve. Impatience is also a big factor.

The best advice I can give you is to have a long-term vision. Have a ten-year plan. Good things don't happen overnight. The seed you plant now will help you get to where you want in years to come. Did you know it takes eighteen months to grow just one pineapple? Have this image in your mind when you first plant your first investments. It might take a year or two before you see it grow at all, but over time it will.

This is a lifelong journey. After I saw my financial adviser with my husband, it really took about five years for everything to fall into place. It certainly didn't happen overnight. It took time before we sold our property, shifted the finances around, and made some lifestyle changes before we saw it was all worth it.

Be patient with yourself and be consistent. Do it even when it feels hard. There were times when I wondered if it was worth the sacrifice. But over time I saw that it definitely was. What begins with small allocations in the beginning can quickly turn into a small fortune a few years later, and you can make yourself independently wealthy as a result.

Start with the basic principles and whatever pool of money you have and build it from there. As long as you have the basic principles in place and you stick to it for the long haul, you will get ahead eventually. These principles are things like putting a percentage of your earnings in savings and investments, diversifying your investments, spending less than you earn, and not relying on credit.

Some people think they are decades away from financial security. You might be shocked to realise that you're closer than you think. And with a bit of work, you're going to get there. Financial freedom can be yours. But it definitely pays to have a long-term vision. Go back to your ten-year plan in Chapter 1.

Ask Questions and Trust the Experts
What you don't understand, you will fear – and that goes for managing your money and investing. Many people are afraid of it, so they don't do it. It is a big reason why people don't seek financial advice. It feels unfamiliar to them, so they don't go there.

This is your opportunity to nip any fear in the bud and be confident in your abilities to own your finances and to get someone who is knowledgeable to help you out. If you don't know much about managing money or growing wealth, you can leave it up to the experts to manage your finances for you. It is okay to let others do the legwork and figure out what will work best for you. That's why you pay them. You can sit back while they do the work for you.

If you were looking for a sign to bite the bullet, this is it.

Whether it is by seeking out a financial adviser or doing some online learning to hone your own money skills – or even talking about money more openly to everyone around you – you're creating financial flashpoints and taking the step toward positive action that will change where you end up financially.

The best thing you can do is talk about it. Talk to friends, family, coworkers, experts, and other people you know and trust. You might be surprised by what they know about finances and investing. Keep searching for answers and ask the right people for guidance so you can ease the stress around money. Once you have a plan of attack for your finances and the right people supporting you, everything starts to look better, and you can take a deep sigh of relief. When things are in place, it will just work like a smooth operation.

> A BEAUTIFUL LIFE CAN GROW FROM ANY MESS. JUST TRUST IN NEW BEGINNINGS AND BELIEVE YOU CAN HAVE MORE. THE BEST IS YET TO COME.

HAVE A TRANSPARENT CONVERSATION WITH A FINANCIAL ADVISER

It's important to have some upfront conversations with your financial adviser. First, you want to make sure they're the right fit for you before you trust them with your money. You also want to make sure they have your best interests at heart and know your life goals.

Firstly, make sure they are qualified and the right fit for you. I've listed the top ten questions to ask your financial adviser earlier on in the chapter, but here is a recap:

- What are your credentials?

- How long have you been a financial adviser, and are you certified?

- How do you charge for your services? What is this going to cost me?

- What's your specialty that you can offer advice on?

- What type of clients do you typically work with?

- How do you think you can help me?

- How often would we see each other?

- How will you manage my money?

Here are some questions advisers hear every day. The answers, however, depend very much on your goals.

- How much do I really need in superannuation to retire comfortably?

- What strategies will help me save more?

- How can I get myself out of debt or reduce the debt I have?

- How can I make better financial decisions to be better off now and in the future?

- Should I buy a house and get out of renting?'

- How can I afford a house?

- How can I get started with investing?

Find out how your adviser can help you personally. You might have other questions to ask them, but here is a starting point.

- How can you help me with my retirement plan?

- How can you help me with my long-term life plan and goals?

- How can I stay on top of my cash flow and expenses?

- How long would it take us to pay off our credit cards and never rack them up again?

- How can we create an emergency savings buffer?

- How can we put away for our kids' future?

- How much fun money do we really need to live a good life every month?

- What other investments can we add to the mix, and how much should we invest?

- What's our plan for life insurance, estate planning, and our wills?

Make a list of some other questions you want to ask your financial adviser, and don't hold back! They are there to help you.

CONTINUING THE CONVERSATION

THIS JOURNEY IS LIFELONG AND DOESN'T STOP HERE.
LET'S KEEP TALKING.

Whether you're now being more honest with yourself and your partner, having talks with your parents or your kids about inheritance or retirement planning, or opening up about money with your friends, colleagues, and even strangers, you've made some huge shifts for the better.

If you've started to think differently about money, this is just the beginning of an exciting lifelong journey. Hopefully you've had some big financial flashpoints along the way that have led you to taking action. You might also come back to some of these chapters at other times in your life.

You have everything you need to have open conversations that will remove the taboo of talking about money and lower the barriers that have been holding you back from living the life you really want. Putting an end to the stigma attached to money starts with you and everyone else around you continuing to have open conversations about money. Not shutting off about money with your friends, your colleagues, your boss, your parents, your partner, and your kids will make everyone feel more comfortable about it.

Just never stop that honest conversation with yourself. It's the most important one.

Talking about money is really about talking about life. Thinking about all the things we care about, our values, and what we want to do with our life.

> MONEY IS THE TOOL THAT ENABLES US TO LIVE OUT OUR DREAMS.

When it comes to achieving your dreams, all I can suggest you do is to aim big, but be real and think long-term. Have a vision that's ten years into the future, so you can realistically achieve what you want in life on your terms. Take moments to think of something good that can happen in the future, and ask yourself how you can make that happen.

Remember to stick to your own path and not let what other people are doing distract you. Think about your own legacy and what you want to leave behind when you're gone. How do you want to authentically live your life now and in the future? And what do you want to be remembered for?

If you can take some time to really reflect on your life so far, and the things that have brought you joy and the things that haven't, then you can start prioritising more joy in the years to come and the time you have left and reduce the things that bring you unhappiness. No matter your responsibilities or who else you are looking after, you deserve to pursue joy and happiness. This is not something that can be done just by taking a holiday, then living as you normally do. It's about really reflecting on what gives you joy and happiness and trying to eliminate the things that don't.

The problem is, we desire money just as much as we hold shame around it. We obsess about it as much as we ignore the problems around it. There's joy in money as much as there is resentment and disappointment. We want more of it, and then we spend it before we think twice about why we worked so hard for it.

Don't hold back when the topic of salary comes up with your friends, colleagues, or boss, or if you're questioning why your friends can drive around in swish new cars when you've been hauling around the same Toyota people mover for years. Talk with your friends about growing wealth and ask them what they're investing in and if they know what the hell cryptocurrency is. You could tell them about what your financial plans are too. Why not?

Because of what I do for a living, I have always had very open dialogue with my close friends around money, as well as my husband, kids, and parents. They know when things are going well for me and when things are tough because I am open about it. And they tell me the same. Sharing your successes and failures with others brings you closer and allows you to have more empathy and understand their state of mind.

It's okay to be vulnerable and to start telling the truth to friends, family, and other people who are close to you that you trust. The more you take ownership of your own money journey and be honest with others who want the best for you – and listen to what they've got to say too – the sooner you can start to really move toward your goals.

Finally, stop worrying about money. Worrying about money is toxic. It takes away your sleep, your joy, and your peace of mind. Instead of worrying about money, put your energy into focusing on it in a positive way. Take control of it and let it work for you, not the other way around.

Use the excitement of imagining the life you want to propel yourself into action to get what you actually want. My hope is that you listen to your heart instead of your doubts and fears.

You have permission to be, do, and have whatever you want. *Whatever you want.* Now take all those financial flashpoints you've sparked and go do it.

Believe that the best is yet to come.

HAVE A COURAGEOUS CONVERSATION ABOUT
MONEY WITH YOUR FRIENDS AND COLLEAGUES

I dare you to have some vulnerable and awkward conversations with your friends and colleagues about money! What could really go wrong?

This doesn't need to be serious. Have fun with it! If you really want to, make a night of it and have a few drinks while you're at it. Red wine isn't going to solve your problems, but it might get you (and them) to open up a bit more. Let's get talking about all this stuff!

Here are some talking points if you need them. You could write these questions on bits of paper and draw them out of a hat, or just randomly shoot them out as icebreakers. You might also decide to just sit down with a friend over a cup of coffee and get talking about money.

- If we're out for dinner and you're not drinking or didn't eat as much as the others, should you pay an evenly split bill?

- Do you think it's unfair that some people get paid way more than others even though they work roughly the same hours? What about the gender pay gap between men and women?

- Who does their taxes on time, and who uses an accountant?

- Has anyone consulted a financial adviser, and did it help?

- Who invests in the stock market? Who's into cryptocurrency?

- What's a blockchain and what's an NTF?

- How do you figure out which ETF or index fund to trade in?

- Any tips on where to start when it comes to investing in the stock market?

- How can you buy overseas stocks?

- How much money should you invest in stocks?

- How much are you setting aside for retirement?

$\longrightarrow$

- What is the number one thing you'd want that money can buy?

- What's the thing for you that you wish money could buy?

- What do you spend too much money on without telling your partner?

- When a parcel arrives from an online shopping purchase, do you feel guilty or happy?

- How much do you really want to be earning and why?

- What's the biggest financial mistake you've ever made, and how have you recovered from it?

- If money wasn't an obstacle, what would you really be doing with your life?

All the answers you will receive on these will start fascinating conversations. Why don't you try it and see what you learn? There are no right or wrong answers when it comes to talking about money. Talking can only improve what you already know.

You've got this!

ACKNOWLEDGEMENTS

There are many people to thank because, without their help, this book would not have happened.

Firstly, to writer, journalist, and my collaboration partner, Kathy Skantzos. Those long conversations, laughs, and tears we have shared creating this book will always be remembered.

To my publisher, Lou Johnson, working with you has been a dream come true. Can't wait for the next twenty.

To my colleague and friend Catherine Weinress, you are valuable beyond measure, and Ann Flanagan, without whom my life would not be near as well organised. Thank you.

To my dear mother, Sue, who has been my biggest supporter, but also my first and only investor in my business. You are loved and appreciated more than I can ever say.

And finally to my husband, Woody, who has always been my partner on this wild ride called life, and my three sons, Sebastian, Connor, and Harrison. You are the reason for it all.

ABOUT THE AUTHOR

Vanessa Stoykov is on a mission to help everyone get real about money.

With over two decades of experience in the wealth creation space, Vanessa knows how important it is to have courageous conversations in order to achieve financial freedom.

From her more-than-twenty-year history of owning a financial services education-focused media business, Evolution Media Group, Vanessa has a deep understanding of the finance world and has the unique ability to communicate this in a way that everyday people can understand.

Through storytelling, and creating engaging and educational content without the jargon, Vanessa helps Australians make better money decisions.

She is also the Founder of NMP Education, creator of the international award-winning TV series *Secrets of The Money Masters: The Investment Series*, and the author of bestselling book *The Breakfast Club for 40-Somethings*.

Vanessa regularly appears in the media, including *Sunrise*, news.com.au, the *Sydney Morning Herald*, ABC News, and *The Today Show* as a financial educator. She is also a member of Chief Executive Women (CEW).

Together with her creative husband, Paul (Woody), Vanessa has three sons and knows firsthand the importance of telling money stories that matter.

Find out more about Vanessa at vanessastoykov.com.au.

ABOUT THE AUTHOR

REFERENCES

For more information about my first book and additional resources you can use that are mentioned in this book, go to Vanessastoykov.com.

The Global Wealth Transfer:

The Greatest Wealth Transfer in History: What's Happening and What Are the Implications, Mark Hall, Nov 11, 2019, sourced from www.forbes.com/sites/markhall/2019/11/11/the-greatest-wealth-transfer-in-history-whats-happening-and-what-are-the-implications/?sh=37dc9ba34090.

What the coming $68 trillion Great Wealth Transfer means for financial advisers, Andrew Osterland, Oct 21 2019, sourced from www.cnbc.com/2019/10/21/what-the-68-trillion-great-wealth-transfer-means-for-advisors.html.

What the Great Wealth Transfer Means For the Economy, Eric Reed, March 14 2020, sourced from finance.yahoo.com/news/great-wealth-transfer-means-economy-233527772.html.

www.euromoney.com/article/b1n0rl4jwqpvx8/generation-next-and-the-great-wealth-transfer.

East to West: Lessons from the global generational wealth transfer, Max Eppel, 27/08/2021, sourced from www.institutionalassetmanager.co.uk/2021/08/27/305399/east-west-lessons-global-generational-wealth-transfer.

www.vanguard.com.au/personal/education-centre/en/insights-article/biggest-wealth-transfer-in-history.

www.lexology.com/library/detail.aspx?g=2e16f159-0341-4f6c-bc51-6a6c041ac5e1.

www.wealthx.com/five-countries-largest-wealth-transfers.

www.hubbis.com/article/asia-s-great-wealth-transfer-implications-for-the-wealth-management-community.

Wealth Tsunami in Australia:
www.news.com.au/finance/money/wealth/baby-boomers-expected-to-leave-wealth-tsunami-of-320000-to-kids/news-story/f86d36a907665588bdfdccc06a981c55.

Superannuation, retirement and inheritance: Reinvention is the New Retirement, No More Practice Education, Griffith University, 2017, sourced from secretsofthemoneymasters.com/wp-content/uploads/2019/08/Reinvention-is-the-New-Retirement-eBook-from-The-Investment-Series.pdf.

www.news.com.au/finance/superannuation/how-much-superannuation-you-need-at-your-age-to-retire-comfortably/news-story/2eedbf7c017c8f84e8f24954404b7ad8.

Financial Literacy:
melbourneinstitute.unimelb.edu.au/__data/assets/pdf_file/0009/3537441/HILDA-Statistical-report-2020.pdf.

rff-dev.ectostarservers.com/forums-archive/evidence-and-innovation-for-scaling-inclusive-digital-finance-rffvi.

gflec.org/wp-content/uploads/2015/11/3313-Finlit_Report_FINAL-5.11.16.pdf?x63881.

Debt:
IMF, global debt: blogs.imf.org/2021/12/15/global-debt-reaches-a-record-226-trillion.

US debt: www.thebalance.com/the-u-s-debt-and-how-it-got-so-big-3305778.

US debt by 2029: www.forbes.com/sites/mikepatton/2021/05/03/
us-national-debt-expected-to-approach-89-trillion-by-
2029/?sh=6f15ae05f13b.

Australia's debt: www.finder.com.au/australias-personal-debt-
reported-as-highest-in-the-world.

Mango Publishing, established in 2014, publishes an eclectic list of books by diverse authors — both new and established voices — on topics ranging from business, personal growth, women's empowerment, LGBTQ+ studies, health, and spirituality to history, popular culture, time management, decluttering, lifestyle, mental wellness, aging, and sustainable living. We were recently named 2019 *and* 2020's #1 fastest-growing independent publisher by *Publishers Weekly.* Our success is driven by our main goal, which is to publish high-quality books that will entertain readers as well as make a positive difference in their lives.

Our readers are our most important resource; we value your input, suggestions, and ideas. We'd love to hear from you — after all, we are publishing books for you!

Please stay in touch with us and follow us at:

Facebook: Mango Publishing
Twitter: @MangoPublishing
Instagram: @MangoPublishing
LinkedIn: Mango Publishing
Pinterest: Mango Publishing
Newsletter: mangopublishinggroup.com/newsletter

Join us on Mango's journey to reinvent publishing, one book at a time.